PRAISE FOR *THE LEADERSHIP CRASH COURSE*

"The Leadership Crash Course *is a clear and lively primer on becoming a great leader. Illustrated with case studies, the book avoids* .... *practical steps to creating value. Anyone in a senior* .... *n Paul Taffinder'*:
Brent Hoberman, CE ...

"Leadership is key in successful corporations. Paul Taffinder's Crash Course *is an excellent hands-on guide for leaders in the real world; facing real world challenges …a must for every executive."*
JW Marriott, Jr, Chairman and CEO, Marriott International, Inc.

"Paul Taffinder's Crash Course *makes excellent reading for whoever wants to reflect on leadership. It is based on real-life experiences and provides valuable hints on how to improve."*
Andre Bergen, CEO, KBC Group

"Paul Taffinder's Leadership Crash Course *distils the elusive concept of leadership into an indispensable practical primer of realistic steps and compelling case studies."*
Robin Paxton, Managing Director, Discovery Networks Europe

"This is excellent. A book that gets to the nub of critical leadership issues… really thought-provoking and insightful, even for the most experienced managers."
Tracy Robbins, Executive Vice President Global Human Resources, Intercontinental Hotels Group

"Neatly clarifies the issues, illustrating them with good case studies from industry."
The Times Educational Supplement

"Contains practical tips on taking a new leadership role and managing change."
People Management

"Paul Taffinder is a respected name in corporate transformation… This book will help you know if you've got what it takes."
Carol Kennedy, *Director Magazine*

THE
LEADERSHIP
CRASH COURSE

THE
LEADERSHIP
CRASH COURSE

HOW TO CREATE PERSONAL LEADERSHIP VALUE

SECOND EDITION

PAUL TAFFINDER

KOGAN PAGE

London and Philadelphia

Publisher's note
Every possible effort has been made to ensure that the information contained in this book is accurate at the time of going to press, and the publishers and authors cannot accept responsibility for any errors or omissions, however caused. No responsibility for loss or damage occasioned to any person acting, or refraining from action, as a result of the material in this publication can be accepted by the editor, the publisher or the author.

First published in 2000
Reprinted in 2000 and 2001
Second edition published in Great Britain and the United States 2006

Apart from any fair dealing for the purposes of research or private study, or criticism or review, as permitted under the Copyright, Designs and Patents Act 1988, this publication may only be reproduced, stored or transmitted, in any form or by any means, with the prior permission in writing of the publishers, or in the case of reprographic reproduction in accordance with the terms and licences issued by the CLA. Enquiries concerning reproduction outside these terms should be sent to the publishers at the undermentioned addresses:

120 Pentonville Road
London N1 9JN
United Kingdom
www.kogan-page.co.uk

525 South 4th Street, #241
Philadelphia PA 19147
USA

© Paul Taffinder, 2000, 2006

The right of Paul Taffinder to be identified as the author of this work has been asserted by him in accordance with the Copyright, Designs and Patents Act 1988.

ISBN 0 7494 4638 2

British Library Cataloguing-in-Publication Data

A CIP record for this book is available from the British Library.

Library of Congress Cataloging-in-Publication Data

Taffinder, Paul.
   The leadership crash course : how to create personal leadership value / Paul Taffinder. – 2nd ed.
      p. cm.
   ISBN 0-7494-4638-2
   1. Leadership. 2. Management. I. Title.
HD57.7.T338 2006
658.4'092--dc22
                              2005033268

Typeset by Jean Cussons Typesetting, Diss, Norfolk
Printed and bound in Great Britain by Thanet Press Ltd, Margate

To the memory of my father, Jack Taffinder.
Always a leader to me.

Contents

Preface

The Leadership Crash Course was first released in 2000. In the eight years preceding that, I had researched and written two books – one on leadership, the other on large-scale change in organizations. During that time, a common theme emerged in my conversations with clients, readers and colleagues, whether they were CEOs or Chief Finance Officers of globe-straddling businesses, mid-level managers in local operations in Spain or South Africa, investment bankers on Wall Street or in London, or the administrators of sprawling government institutions the world over. Typically the letter, e-mail or conversation would run something like: 'I've been to training courses on leadership. I've read dozens of books. I've thought about the great leaders – Alexander the Great, Churchill, Mahatma Gandhi, Patton, Nelson, Napoleon, Mandela. It's all fascinating – in theory – but how do I apply it to me, to my situation now in a practical, down-to-earth way?' What was startling to me was how similar these views were at every level of every organization. You would expect young, ambitious supervisors to openly ask for help as they developed their leadership potential but mid- and senior-level executives were seeking the same pragmatic support and insight about the actions they should take, the behaviour they needed to develop and the things they should focus on. What they did not want was more theory or more lessons from the lives of the gifted 'Great Leaders' like those mentioned above, whose very greatness made them both remote and impossible to emulate.

All this was happening at a time when the demand for genuine leadership was reaching a crescendo, swept along by globalization, unremitting competition between businesses, the privatization of whole tranches of government institutions, from airlines to electricity to water companies, and driven on by customers and shareholders who, in their own different ways, wanted to maximize the value they received. If that was the external landscape, the internal battleground was one in which supervisors, managers and executives felt, at the same time, excited and exposed. If you could build your leadership capabilities, you could have greater impact, your troops could achieve more and your career prospects were tremendous. On the other hand, the pressure to perform as a leader left many people confused and unsure how to apply the theories and models of leadership in practical, day-to-day ways.

A suggestion from a board executive I was advising got things started. 'What we need here,' he said, 'is a practical work-book, a course-by-course guide that gets us to *do* the leadership you keep telling us about.' *The Leadership Crash Course* was born.

The intention behind the book was, and still is, to encourage people to fix in their minds a simple, challenging leadership model and then take the personal risk of applying each of the five elements of leadership behaviour in their everyday work. It was not, and still isn't, a book aimed only at chief executives running large businesses; rather, as the board executive above made clear, *The Crash Course* was to be a series of modules that individuals at many levels could study, deploy in their departments or businesses, or simply use as a reminder from time to time of what leadership was really about. In addition, the layout of the book is geared towards action – reading, assessing your own behaviour and then trying things. It is also a book that requires you to be honest with yourself: if you refuse to see and measure your true strengths and weaknesses as a leader, you will have wasted your time reading it. The leadership model and the approach of the book seemed to strike a chord – and not only in the English-speaking world. Requests for editions in Spanish, Portuguese, German, Korean, Chinese, Polish and Latvian demonstrated, somewhat to my surprise, the international clamour for a pragmatic, challenging book on leadership, in spite of the received wisdom on the gulf between national cultures. Equally, my opportunities for dialogue with people across the world have multiplied, and if on the one hand their need for a book like *The Crash Course* is still unchanged, on the other hand their feedback to me suggests a slightly different emphasis for this new edition. This is best captured in the question: 'How do I exert greater impact as a leader?'

The obvious, but poorly reasoned, answer is for leaders to do more of the same, or perhaps more passionately or on a bigger stage... but I feel this misses the point. And it occurred to me that as leadership in action is almost always about dilemmas, difficult choices and asking risky questions, perhaps this wasn't quite the right question. Impact is important: it creates motive power, the energy to awaken people to surprising opportunities and ambitions. But, on its own, impact is somewhat sterile. It doesn't necessarily create value. And it was the word 'value' that challenged my thinking the most. A reworking of the above question was therefore needed, if it was to challenge and really develop both established and aspirant leaders.

The question therefore became: 'How do I create value through my leadership?' It is a complex question and there may be multiple definitions of what constitutes value in different types of human enterprise, but it is also a universal leadership question which gets at the fundamentals of why a leader, at whatever level and in whichever circumstance, might act the way he or she does. So that is the challenge of this new edition of *The Crash Course* and, of course, your challenge as its reader.

There have been other changes to the book. There are more case studies and updated war stories on leaders. In addition, building on some ongoing psycho-metric work I and others have done on how individual leaders tend to fall into dominant patterns of behaviour, I have added a final chapter, Course 7. This sets out the most common leadership 'sub-domains' and typical behavioural compo-nents of leaders, including the blind spots and dangers associated with each.

Finally, over the years I have had a huge range of comments and feedback on one particular component of the leadership domain – *Unpredictability*. People have always reacted strongly to the title, something I take as a good sign since the word's power provokes intense reaction and a deeper engagement with what leadership really means. However, like many people, I myself have always been both pleased and slightly uncomfortable with what the word conveys – pleased because it asks leaders to be different, restless, change-oriented, prepared to chal-lenge, to be adventurous; uncomfortable because it also conveys a sense of the capricious, of vacillation, inconstancy or even being irresolute. These latter behav-ioural qualities run directly counter to the power of leadership and its value. It was no easy decision but I listened to the feedback and have made the change: *Unpredictability* has become *Challenge and Change*.

Writing this as we begin 2006 and reflecting on the intervening years since *The Crash Course* was first released, I find that the need for leadership is more urgent, more important. This need is self-evident. In the political sphere it is signified in the great events that have shaped the start of the 21st century: global warming, 9/11, the Palestinian *Intifada*, the wars in Afghanistan and Iraq, the war on terror and the war on poverty. In economics it is the rise of India and China as commercial powerhouses and the impact of technology and vast capital movements in driving globalization and lowering barriers to entry. And in the organizational world it is the intensity of competitive pressure, ongoing mergers and acquisitions, the collapse and integration of once separate industries and businesses, and the blurring of the lines between government and private sector. In all of these events and processes, leadership is intimately and decisively the difference between excellence and mediocrity, success and failure.

Acknowledgements

My thanks are due to…

First and foremost, Mandy, without whom…

And also Alan and Nick who are still doing their best to distract me: Al, I'm waiting for a 50; Nick, straight bat;

Jon Lurie, for good advice and all the schoolboy humour;

Ken Favaro, Ron Langford, Herman Spruit, Matt Symonds, Rob McKinnon and Simon Kenyon for making me feel welcome, offering the unique Marakon perspective and some helpful ideas; Julie-Anne Boxall for helping to get things organized; my editor at Kogan Page, Pauline Goodwin, for suggesting and having faith in a new edition, and her team for pulling it all together.

1 Be a manager or a leader

Key action list and course objectives

- To understand the difference between managing and leading people.
- To assess your own preference for either managing or leading.
- To understand why leadership is so important and valued today.
- To learn how leadership is different in the new globally connected business environment.
- To be clear on how to take the six modules of the Leadership Crash Course.

MODULE 1.1: THE BIG DIFFERENCE

Are you a leader or a manager? Yes, there's a difference, a huge difference. And you need to make a choice about which you want to be. The world is full of managers and desperately short of leaders – real leaders. Organizations all over the world spend hundreds of millions every year training people to be better managers but struggle to develop enough leaders. Sure, we need both managers and leaders – the skills of managing are valuable, indeed essential, in making things happen and keeping work on track – but they are far outweighed by the demand for leadership skills in today's world.

But why? Why this demand for leadership? There are many reasons, not least the massive shifts in the geopolitical landscape of the world after the 9/11 attack on New York's twin towers. In addition there is the ubiquitous pressure of change exerted in every industry, sector and almost all walks of life. Some of this change is expected, even predictable. Witness, for example, the change that comes from outsourcing whole departments such as IT and customer contact centres or the off-shoring of jobs to India and China. Likewise, many employees and managers are well accustomed to quality and customer service 'improvement initiatives' – some of which crop up with monotonous regularity and only rare impact (and, indeed, for reasons that stem largely from poor leadership). On the other hand, the 24/7 interaction of societies and economies that we call globalization, together with the impact of the internet, wireless communications such as Bluetooth, and mobile technology like BlackBerry and iPod, are delivering changes not only to office workers right across industries but also to consumers in every market – teenagers with their music and fashions, schoolchildren in their classrooms and homes, patients in the healthcare system and even politicians with their electorates.

It is also true that as globalization increases, all of the conditions described above make barriers to entry for new competitors easier to overcome. This means that new companies can easily replicate what existing firms already do and may, through lower costs, drive the older companies to the wall. These conditions make leadership even more important – great leaders will inspire their employees and make the tough decisions that create superior economic performance in their companies.

I hazard little in guessing that one of the reasons you have started reading this book is because you yourself are facing a change of some sort or want to introduce change around you, most likely in your work. Psychological research has shown what we all intuitively know: under circumstances of uncertainty or unusual challenge and difficulty, people look for help in understanding questions about what matters, what to do, what direction to take, and what they should not do. Providing people with the answers that help them with these difficult questions is the essence of leadership. And it is only a small step, then, to realize that successful change requires leadership.

MODULE 1.2: CAN I LEARN TO BE A LEADER?

Yes. That's the good news. Anyone can learn leadership skills and can be successful in leading others. That's not to say that it's easy. Nor is there is a simple and mechanistic programme of training that will transform you from a supervisor into a chief executive, from an employee with big ideas into a billionaire entrepreneur, from a talented athlete into an inspirational team coach, or from a government bureaucrat into a charismatic political heavyweight. Learning to be a leader, like most things, takes effort and application, practice and dedication – and not simply training. You don't learn leadership in a classroom. And, most importantly, it takes a particular human quality that turns many people off the challenge: courage, the courage to change yourself, to try things, to experiment, to risk making mistakes and risk failures.

UNCOMFORTABLE LEADERSHIP LESSON NO. 1.
CHANGE YOURSELF BEFORE YOU TRY TO CHANGE OTHERS

I once got to know the CEO of a large international manufacturer with revenues of some $2 billion, operating in dozens of countries worldwide. He had been with the company man and boy, starting in a lowly clerical role but rising through the ranks rapidly and successfully. As CEO he wanted to change the organization before it was swamped by more nimble, bloodthirsty competitors. He wanted the company to become a truly global corporation and communicated his vision to the executive team and the entire organization, expecting that people would get on with the necessary changes.

But nothing happened for nine months, despite his frustration, fury, cajoling and best efforts to set out his vision for the future of the business. Gradually he realized that he would have to change himself before he could get others to change their behaviour and thus change the organization. With real dedication, using coaching, psychometric tests, inventories and feedback from others, he set out to transform himself – from being a high-performance, demanding *manager* to being a real *leader*. Only once he had achieved this change, was it possible for him to begin to change the organization.

You can be the supervisor of a team of two staff or, like the guy in this cautionary tale, the CEO of a huge enterprise employing 20,000 people... and still not be a leader. The measure of true leadership is being able to get people to do things they didn't want to do or didn't expect they could do. But learning to be a leader is about learning to change yourself first before you try to change others.

MODULE 1.3: DO YOU PREFER TO BE A LEADER OR A MANAGER?

Before you can start learning the behaviours, skills, tricks and secrets of leadership, you need to find out what your true preference is. During the course of your development as a person, as you grew up, went to school, started work and so on, you came to behave in ways that were typically *you* – your personality, if you like. For a few people, some of these ways of behaving are exactly the sorts of behaviour that would make them 'natural' leaders – not natural in the sense that they are born leaders (no one is born a leader) but in the sense that they are very comfortable behaving that way. For others, their normal and comfortable ways of behaving are some way off the types of behaviour that make for effectiveness as a leader – in short, they have more to learn. But that doesn't mean they will ultimately be inferior leaders. The very challenge of learning new behaviour and constantly striving to be a better leader can drive these people to excel as leaders.

One quick way of finding out your preference is to complete the Leader/ Manager Inventory in Table 1.1. Be honest. The more open with yourself you are, the quicker you can learn to be a leader. Use the fast scoring guide not only to see what your preference is but also to identify which types of behaviour you are

Table 1.1 *Course 1, Leader/Manager Inventory*

Which of the following is most true of your current behaviour (ie which of the two behaviours do you prefer)? For each of the ten pairs of behaviour, choose either 'a' or 'b'.	
1a Concentrate on the task to get it done ☐	1b Question whether it's the right task ☐
2a Form your own opinion, then listen to others ☐	2b Listen carefully to others' opinions then choose the one you believe in ☐
3a Avoid or minimize risks ☐	3b Take risks ☐
4a Get impatient for urgent progress ☐	4b Make steady progress towards your goal ☐
5a Concentrate more on the task ☐	5b Concentrate more on relationships with people ☐
6a Worry about what you haven't achieved ☐	6b Take pride in what you've already achieved ☐
7a Keep your excitement about a task to yourself ☐	7b Show your excitement about a task ☐
8a Create adventure ☐	8b Create a plan you can control ☐
9a Keep your points of view to yourself ☐	9b Often spend time persuading people to take your point of view ☐
10a Often surprise people ☐	10b Rarely surprise people ☐

Scoring

Give yourself 1 point for each of the following items that you ticked: 1a, 2b, 3a, 4b, 5a, 6b, 7a, 8b, 9a, 10b

Give yourself 2 points for each of the following items that you ticked: 1b, 2a, 3b, 4a, 5b, 6a, 7b, 8a, 9b, 10a

Score 18 or more: You are very comfortable with leadership and probably dislike many of the everyday tasks required to be a good manager. But, don't be complacent: making sure that you can handle, or rely on others around you to handle, the regular management tasks is as important as being an effective leader. Remember too, the best leaders are constantly striving to be better.

Score 13–17: You have a feel for leadership, but struggle at times and need to hone areas of weakness.

Score 12 or less: You prefer managing rather than leading and probably look to others for leadership in most situations, concentrating instead on making progress on tasks and keeping work on track. You have no doubt often asked yourself: 'How can I lead people? What is leadership? How do leaders do it?'

comfortable with and those areas where you may need to expend real effort to develop yourself as a leader.

MODULE 1.4: SO WHAT IS LEADERSHIP?

This is one of those most frequently asked questions – even by chief executives or political commentators. James McGregor Burns, the American political scientist and a staunch campaigner for John F Kennedy in the 1950s and 1960s, made the famous remark that leadership was 'one of the most observed and least understood phenomena on earth'. Many people are anxious for a simple one-line answer and when I'm asked that question, I say three things:

- *The easy answer:* leadership is getting people to do things they have never thought of doing, do not believe are possible or that they do not want to do.
- *The leadership in organizations answer:* leadership is the action of committing employees to contribute their best to the purpose of the organization.
- *The complex (and more accurate) answer:* you only know leadership by its consequences – from the fact that individuals or a group of people start to behave in a particular way as a result of the actions of someone else.

You see, leadership is not always intentional. People often follow the example of someone in authority – even if that person doesn't want them to. Consider the leadership set by parents to their children when they say, 'Don't interrupt when we're talking,' but regularly interrupt each other or their children during conversation. This is a critical lesson both for leaders and for those who aspire to leadership: those you are leading may follow your example (good and bad) and ignore your exhortations.

The true measure of your success as a leader is not the boldness of your intentions, the quality of your presentations and speeches, the strength of your relationships with people, or the extent to which you are liked by your team; rather, it is your success in moving people to follow your lead.

Another way to define leadership is to go back to the difference between managers and leaders that we touched on earlier. This helps to show what your

Table 1.2   *The differences between what leaders and managers do*

Managers	Leaders
Control risks	Take risks
React	Seek opportunities
Enforce organizational rules	Change organizational rules
Seek and then follow direction	Provide something to believe in
Coordinate effort	Inspire achievement

focus of effort should be as a leader. Table 1.2 shows the stark differences between what leaders do and managers do.

Many people in today's organizations rise to senior levels in the hierarchy by being good at managing: they make things happen, they keep things moving, they deliver results, they watch costs and produce efficiencies. Indeed, some of these people are what I call 'high-performance managers': they are truly fantastic at being managers, they impress the people who work for them, earn the praise of their peers and bosses and rise rapidly up the management ladder. But they are unable to lead: regrettably, in enterprises where there is a preponderance of high-performance managers, the organizational culture tends to fall into a spiral of being over-managed and under-led, becoming a place of navel-gazing, resistant to change and focused on the wrong strategic direction and priorities. Such enterprises usually plummet suddenly and, by all appearances, inexplicably into difficulties and sometimes disaster – witness IBM in the late 1980s, Fiat, WorldCom, Apple Computer and Marks & Spencer.

MODULE 1.5: LEADERSHIP VALUE

What is the point of leadership? Why is it so important to people? Why do organizations value it so much? A quick walk through history can help us answer these questions.

Organizing people into a group with a structured form helps people to work in concert to achieve more than they could as individuals or as a loosely interacting social entity. Civilization as a whole is founded on the notion of structure and organization of people and their efforts. You see its application all around you in hospitals, schools, workplaces, civil institutions, construction, religion, politics, sport and the military. This concept has been appreciated for 3,000 years and even in deepest antiquity it was applied in the very earliest societies and it helped propel many of them to astonishing pre-eminence. To take just a single example: the Roman army (modelled on the Greek hoplite armies before it) understood that a mob of warriors without structure and order was much less effective than one divided into lines of infantry and subdivided into units of 120–60 soldiers, with a clear chain of command.

The Romans, like their forebears, also knew that individual 'leaders' made a huge, sometimes crucial, difference to the incremental value that structure and organization offered. This value was usually defined as 'morale' or 'pride' or 'courage' and was most vividly measured in battle when even outnumbered or poorly organized troops might be inspired to unlikely valour and sacrifice, winning victory against the odds.

No rational argument or appeal to logic could induce this kind of behaviour. In battle, under terrifying threat, the most natural course of action was to flee and the sudden rout of an army was fairly common. To prevent it and to go beyond it to bolster confidence and even eagerness to engage in battle required more than organization and structure – particularly when the odds were obviously against you. In its purest sense, therefore, the motive force of leadership acts at the emotional and sometimes irrational level. This makes the development of a rational formula to 'deliver' leadership elusive – though not unreachable.

Are things any different in today's world? Not really. Perhaps the scale of human enterprise is greater, the connectedness of different institutions and cultural groups stronger and the pace of work and life much faster. But structure and organization are still very important. And the value that individual leaders create is still paramount. Against the odds, Nelson Mandela helped transform a whole country. And in a less historic manner, individual leaders all over the world make a difference by:

- persuading disparate factions to pursue common cause;
- providing a sense of achievement and motivation to succeed that structure and organization cannot;

- calling on commitment to action or even sacrifice by individuals to benefit the team or enterprise;
- inspiring people to overcome seemingly impossible obstacles;
- creating excitement and ambition to perform at a higher level;
- engendering hope among people who are despairing.

What you will notice about this list is that *the value leadership creates is both subjective and practical.* Indeed, for almost everyone in the world, it is subjective experiences that are the most important for them – the feeling of confidence that comes of having overcome impossible odds, the dignity of contributing to a meaningful or important enterprise, the sense of achievement in success or learning something new, the satisfaction of having done the best for one's family, team or business or having gained the esteem of colleagues. At the same time, leadership value is intensely practical – because it moves things forward, it creates action, it changes the world, it increases the likelihood of growth, attainment and success.

This leadership value, however, is greatest when leadership behaviour is most closely aligned with or in support of a higher purpose – that of the group, the organization, the enterprise, the country. A perfect example of this is outlined in the Lloyds TSB story that follows, showing how Sir Brian Pitman transformed the bank's fortunes with his clear articulation of new purpose.

In fact leadership value is *generally* and *specifically* about purpose. In the general sense this is because, for leaders to be successful, they must offer people (their followers) a goal to pursue, a task to accomplish, a greater ambition to achieve. However, in the specific sense, leaders must perform a difficult trick – they must coherently and convincingly link an individual's actions, aspirations and hopes, in tandem with the actions, aspirations and hopes of tens, hundreds or even thousands of other individuals, to this overarching purpose.

SIR BRIAN PITMAN AND LLOYDS TSB

When Sir Brian Pitman became chief executive of Lloyds TSB, the bank was one of the least valuable banks in the world. By 1997 he had transformed it into the world's most valuable bank, with a market capitalization of $70 billion.

Sir Brian cleared away the multiple and confusing goals that were hobbling the bank's performance and introduced a single overarching objective of maximizing the intrinsic value of the company. The strategy that would deliver this overall objective was simple but, at the time, ran wildly counter to prevailing business wisdom: instead of remaining a full-service bank with a portfolio of diversified businesses that spread and therefore reduced financial risk, Lloyds would focus on the markets where the bank was strong and attract and serve customers neglected by competitors.

To execute this strategy meant that as a leader Sir Brian would have to sustain, through criticism, scepticism and outright resistance from many executives and employees, a devotion to the bank's new objective and strategy - encouraging, inspiring, cajoling and driving executives and managers to focus their attention, efforts and resources on the opportunities that would deliver both customer value and short- and long-term performance for shareholders.

MODULE 1.6: THE LEADERSHIP DOMAIN... OR HOW TO BE A LEADER

Leadership is about getting people to achieve new things, and therefore largely about change – about inspiring, helping and, yes, sometimes enforcing, change in people. There are five critical areas that I have identified during my work with leaders and in the research I have done on the subject (see, for example, my book *The New Leaders*, 1995, published by Kogan Page, or *Big Change*, 1998, published by Wiley). As a leader you must:

- impose or set the context (making it clear what matters);
- make risks and take risks;
- challenge and change;
- have deep conviction;
- generate critical mass (make things happen at scale).

That's the high-level view of what leadership is. Now we need to look at each of these areas in more detail.

Imposing context

First off, *imposing context* means you must make it absolutely clear what is important in the enterprise, what its direction and goals are, where it has come from and where it is going, what your values as the leader are and, by extension, how they fit with the values of the enterprise, and therefore what is expected of your people. I call this *imposing context* because people need a framework within which to live, work and achieve. Without this, human beings either stick slavishly to the humdrum and mundane, achieving little, or their individuality draws them into haphazard, directionless competition with each other.

Many managers in organizations make the mistake of believing that leadership is primarily about vision – that is, about setting a future direction. This is wrong! Certainly people need to know what direction to take, where their future lies or what they might aspire to, but this over-focus on the future neglects two elements crucial to people: their *history* and where they are now. Individuals rarely understand what action to take or how they should change unless they can perceive the thread that links a vision of the future with their current situation as well as where they have come from. More on this in Course 2. For the moment think of imposing context as the rules of the game – as *they were, as they are and as they will be in the future.*

Table 1.3   *Leaders impose context*

What	How	Why
As a leader you must: *Impose context…*	by concentrating people's attention on what matters…	in order to: ● give people a direction to take or an aspiration to pursue ● show individuals what the key goals are ● make sure people always have a sense of proportion and can distinguish day-to-day between what actions are important and those that are not

Table 1.4   *Leaders make risks and take risks*

What	How	Why
As a leader you must: *Make risks and take risks...*	by understanding what opportunities exist, or can be created, and then converting them into results...	in order to: ● pre-empt the otherwise hidden or unexpected risks that might damage the enterprise ● take advantage of opportunities for success in the present or future ● create new ways of doing things that are beneficial, advantageous or profitable ● expose yourself and your people to new situations that develop thinking and skills

Make risks and take risks

Second, leaders are distinguished by their ability to *make and take risks* – that is, to both seek out and create opportunities and then turn these opportunities into advantages or results. A senior executive put it this way to me: 'I always say, if you're not making mistakes, you're not *doing* anything!' This means asking questions about what needs to change, taking risks on new business ventures or new strategic directions, freeing people to try new things, giving energetic individuals the chance to prove themselves and develop, seeking out your people's creative ideas and innovations and letting them have a go.

But, and this is a big but, *risk making and risk taking* is not a prescription or excuse for sloppy, lazy management. Risk *can* and *should* go hand-in-hand with management rigour and discipline. How? Well, leadership risk creates opportunities while management rigour turns them into tangible results.

Table 1.5   *Leaders must challenge and change*

What	How	Why
As a leader you must: *Challenge and change...*	by experimenting and being adventurous...	in order to: ● grab people's attention ● energize your followers ● take competitors by surprise ● jolt your people, from time to time, out of accepting things as they are, to prevent the ordinary becoming all that they believe is possible

Challenge and change

Third, it is true in many organizations and enterprises that people are fearful, apathetic, cynical, sceptical, stuck in a rut, or simply trapped in the workaday grind of the status quo. This is a difficulty for would-be leaders at most times, but is especially fraught when the enterprise is facing large-scale, radical change. You will have heard the comments, perhaps even been moved to utter them yourself: 'It's been done before. It'll never work. It can't be done.'

So what is a leader to do when faced with such a mountain of granite scepticism or indifference? The answer: do something different. Be unpredictable. Do what no one expects. Surprise people. Ask your people to challenge you and change the way things are done. Blow them out of their ruts. *Challenge and change.*

Have deep conviction

Perhaps the most distinctive mark of leaders is their *conviction*. They believe wholeheartedly in what they're doing, but that alone is not enough. If you have deep conviction but never show it, you cannot lead others. Leaders demonstrate their conviction. They talk about what they want to achieve and they reveal their

Table 1.6 *Leaders have deep conviction*

What	How	Why
As a leader you must: *Have deep conviction...*	by being fervent about the things you want to achieve...	in order to: ● guide your decisions ● inspire people to follow you ● overcome the inevitable barriers and obstacles ● have the courage to stand your ground ● build self-belief in your people

emotional involvement in it by showing their excitement, their impatience, and their determination.

None the less, aspiring leaders frequently confuse conviction with never changing their minds. They think that they have to have an answer for everything and make an instant decision. Leaders *do* change their mind, but once they commit to a decision, they put their conviction on the line. The epithets I would use to describe leaders who have true conviction are: single-minded, excited by the future, fervent, determined, totally resolved. Think about yourself: do you demonstrate these qualities? If not, why not?

Generate critical mass

No matter how much conviction you have, no matter how rapidly and effectively you mobilize your people and get them to commit to achieving aspirational goals, no matter what risks you take – if you fail to channel the available energy of a group of people into tasks that make a difference, that make things happen, then you will have failed the toughest test of leadership. Sir Francis Drake put this with great insight when he remarked: 'There must be a beginning of any great matter, but the continuing unto the end, until it be thoroughly finished, yields the true glory.'

It is the leadership skills of *generating critical mass* that enable you to push your people beyond simply starting new initiatives (but never finishing them), or working on multiple tasks (that are uncoordinated), or putting enormous effort into activities (but the wrong activities). This also requires you to influence people – to get them to do things they may not want to do, to join you in achieving something that is not self-evidently in their own interests, to adjust their viewpoint or their ideals and fall in behind you. Too many managers these days still believe they can operate within a command and control framework where their people will meekly do as they're told.

Employees, especially the younger generation of employees, are less inclined to take a job for life, are better educated and have higher expectations. They respond poorly to command and control. Their creativity and their positive emotional response to customers are better released through influence, persuasion and involvement. This is doubly and trebly true of 'knowledge workers' – those who are employed specifically for the knowledge they bring to the job and the organization. And it is the lifeblood of leadership of the growing cadre of 'star performers' – those individuals and teams whose efforts produce massive returns: sports people, pop stars, script-writers, investment analysts and traders, leading-edge software developers and the like.

Table 1.7   *Leaders generate critical mass*

What	How	Why
As a leader you must: *Generate critical mass...*	by influencing people and turning knowledge into action...	in order to: ● channel your people's energy into the appropriate activities ● mobilize all your people to work together in a coordinated way (rather than in an individualistic, haphazard manner) ● make things happen

MODULE 1.7: LEADERSHIP BY E-MAIL

Leadership nowadays is made more complex (if you hadn't already noticed) by the advance of new technologies. We hear a lot about the '24/7 globally connected world' these days. New technologies such as e-mail, the internet, web tools, blogging, instant messaging, texting and Bluetooth have produced extraordinary breakthroughs in human performance and productivity as well as reducing the cost and speed of transacting business. In addition, geography has shrunk: it is easy to deliver multiple types of services seamlessly from different corners of the globe. Consider just a few examples:

- 24-hour credit card customer service across time zones, from staff based in Ireland and Canada for US and European customers;
- technical monitoring of office maintenance services (air-conditioning, lifts and so forth) in New York from India;
- simultaneous collaborative design of automotive engines from engineering shops in Detroit, Tokyo and London;
- instant access to the very latest leading-edge advisory work from a database of global client experiences for professionals in Norway who are advising their customer in Moscow.

We hear a lot about the excitement of new technology and how it can improve business effectiveness. Every day we come across ways in which all kinds of human enterprise are improved right across the world. The media especially are fascinated by the applications of new technology. But we hear next to nothing about the difficulties, challenges and real problems created by having to interact with, work with, manage and, most of all, lead people (whom you may have never met) in dispersed locations (whether this is 50 metres or 5,000 kilometres away) via the ubiquitous e-mail.

Obvious Question No. 1: Does e-mail make any difference to the way people interact?
Answer: Yes. Resoundingly, yes! Look at Table 1.8 to see the differences between three types of human interaction: 'normal' face-to-face, telephonic and e-mail.

Table 1.8 *Differences between normal, telephonic and e-mail interaction*

Type of Human Communication	Medium of Interaction		
	Face-to-face	Telephonic	E-mail
Vocabulary (detail of language)	Full range 100% ⇧	Full range 100% ⇧	Medium range 60% ⇧
Tone of voice (expressiveness)	Full range 100% ⇧	Restricted 40% ⇧	Severely restricted 0–20% ⇧
Non-verbal	Full range 100% ⇧	Absent	Absent

Remember, the invention of writing (some 6,000 years ago) made a huge differ-ence to human communication, but most dramatically when Gutenberg's printing press brought the start of mass publishing some 500 years ago. The telephone had a similar impact, changing the nature of work and the type of work that could be done, not to mention the everyday experience of communication.

When face-to-face, we can employ and perceive the full range of important human interactive mechanisms. We can use a vast language vocabulary – thou-sands of words arrayed in multiple types of sentences. We can raise our voices or lower them, talk in a hushed, secretive manner or in a bold, assertive way. We can speak in a tone of disappointment or excitement or scepticism. Face-to-face we can laugh, show our anger and pleasure, and either reinforce this or even deliberately send complex mixed messages by our posture (head down, arms folded, etc) or by our facial expressions (eyes narrowed, tongue-in-cheek, brows raised, eyes rolling and so forth).

The telephone permits the full range of language to be used, although people do interact differently on the telephone than face-to-face. This is because human interaction is dynamic: it is not just about language, but about how we use language through tonal inflection (at its most basic, raising or lowering our voices) and how we display ourselves through the use of our bodies (non-verbal behaviour or body language). The telephones that you use every day depend upon microphone and receiver technology designed (for reasons of cost) to convey only a limited tonal range. In other words, the person listening to you at the end of the phone is not hearing an exact transmission of your voice, merely an approximation. Vitally, while this approximation gives your listener the full range of words you choose to use, it provides only some 40 per cent or less of the complex tonal variations that we use, unthinkingly, every moment of a conversation. It goes without saying, moreover, that the telephone robs us entirely of non-verbal cues. Even television falls short of conveying the complexity of facial and body expression, so the new breed of video phones, as they become more widespread, will not come close to a 100 per cent representation of face-to-face interaction.

In some ways this 'unresponsiveness' of the telephone is a good thing. Human interaction depends on our ability not only to communicate, but also to avoid communicating certain things or getting too intimate. Thus, telephones can add formality and distance in our dealings as customers with large organizations. This can be a good thing when making a complaint, handling tax or legal matters, even dealing with your bank.

E-mail and emotion

The widespread use of e-mail is very different. Look at Table 1.8 again. The range for non-verbal expression is zero and tonal expression is severely curtailed. It is interesting that, because of the need for a greater range of expression in the electronic workspace, people have, in their own inventive ways, gone about creating tonal expression in e-mail by using what are called 'emoticons' – patterns of keystrokes to add tone to the words or denote emotional states. So, for example, the most obvious use of such symbols (borrowed from writing and printing) is italics or underlining to *emphasize* a point or *stress* something. Likewise a sentence in capitals might mean that you are SHOUTING or ANGRY. Just look at the effect of capitalizing. Your eye is drawn. You are, perhaps, startled. The words have been given greater meaning. Further symbols are based on rudimentary facial expression such as :) to denote a funny remark or :(to denote the opposite. Importantly, however, all these symbols are very limited. Indeed, we are most often unsure what the author of an e-mail means by capitalizing or by adding '!!!' at the end of a sentence. They are the somewhat desperate attempt of people to communicate better, ie to convey emotion, make subtle points and so on *under time pressure*.

Face-to-face, we take this ability for granted. People can read our expressions as we talk; we do not have to think about expressions and then turn them on. But these days millions of people worldwide are communicating with each other only by e-mail. Inevitably, miscommunication happens. People misunderstand what is written in their e-mails. And why? Because, although most people can write reasonably well, they do not possess the skills of a Charles Dickens, Leo Tolstoy or Norman Mailer to express emotion subtly and convincingly. But they need to.

STEVIE

Take the case of Stevie. As she took on her new role as Products Relationship Manager for Europe, handling some half-a-dozen clients, she began to receive e-mails from her sales team (numbering 10), the operations people (contact with up to six), her boss, eight country heads and her clients (at least six). She used the phone a lot (landline mostly but mobile when travelling) but needed to see the 'correspondence' on e-mail every day. Volumes of e-mail rose rapidly, hitting 60 or more per day. She could handle the volume because most required replies of only one or two lines.

It was the misunderstandings that alarmed her. Some of her own sales team were at each other's throats, apparently blaming each other for oversights or client problems. Worse, when she began to dig deeper, meeting her clients and her sales team one-to-one, she was amazed to find that people were making judgements about each other based entirely on a couple of e-mails sent in the distant past. On a few occasions, under time pressure, one of the sales representatives had sent an urgent note to a colleague requesting that some missing data be sent to his client as soon as possible – and he had copied the e-mail to his client. The e-mail itself, fresh to Stevie's eyes, seemed innocuous but the use of capitals in one line (PLEASE ATTEND TO THIS URGENTLY!!!) did make it look, well, aggressive. And so it turned out. The recipient of the e-mail had read this as not only aggressive, but rude and, having only met her colleague once or twice at sales conferences in the past, decided that he was not a man she could get on with or could get to know better. The client had interpreted the e-mail as confusion in the ranks of his supplier and was not entirely confident that he would receive an appropriate level of service in future. This particular situation was relatively straightforward to resolve and Stevie did that by getting the two colleagues to work together and get to know each other. Trickier was the realization that confusion of this sort was the tip of the iceberg. What should she do?

Reading this salutary tale, is it any wonder that corporations spend hundreds of millions of dollars every year getting people together, face-to-face, eyeball-to-eyeball? Personal contact is important. Knowing people is important. Trust is important. However, getting to know people and building trust with them is difficult, if not impossible, if you never meet them or, from time to time, renew the face-to-face contact. People prefer to interact and work with others whom they can understand and trust.

Obvious Question No. 2: Do you need to know and trust people to work with them? *Answer:* Yes. Especially where work is based more and more on rapid formation, recombining and break-up of temporary teams, or where change is a constant factor and where you have the advantage to do work faster and more effectively if talented people can collaborate quickly because they already know and trust one another.

Guidelines for leadership by e-mail

In an organization where there is heavy use of e-mail, you can be a better leader by observing the following guidelines:

- *Never assume that, or let yourself drift into an ongoing situation where, e-mail is your prime mode of communication.* Face-to-face is essential, as often as possible, especially when you first take on a leadership role. You must get to know people before using e-mail at high volume. And the best leaders continue to have high levels of personal, eyeball contact with their people, their peers and their bosses.

- *If you have no opportunity for face-to-face interaction, the telephone is a much better alternative to e-mail if you are trying to lead people.* One manager who was very successful with a dispersed workforce used to spend most of his time simply phoning his 45 staff, at least once every couple of days, using the style of, 'How are things going? How can I help? Any problems?' In so doing, he was maintaining and building relationships and regularly reminding people of overall goals and how their work contributed.

- *Use e-mail primarily for rapid communication of essential documents* (eg checking letters, sales reports and so on).

- *Make it clear to your colleagues and staff how you expect e-mail to be used.* Do not take it for granted that people will know what you expect. Lay it out for them in a short list of guidelines and then ensure that you follow the guidelines all the time.

- *Avoid as much as possible the appalling habit of copying dozens of people on each e-mail.* This usually indicates a 'cover-your-ass' syndrome, which needs rapid intervention before it spirals into serious problems where individuals will not take responsibility or are frightened to make a stand or take risks.

- *Where you are using e-mail, be very sensitive to the often alarming emotional readings that recipients make of symbols and emoticons* (discussed above). Take a lesson from the publishing and printing world, which has been dealing with this issue for hundreds of years, and learn that less is more. Keep e-mails short and only use italics or capitals where you want to make a really critical point (and that should not be too often). Encourage your people to do the same.

MODULE 1.8: HOW TO GET THE BEST OUT OF THE LEADERSHIP CRASH COURSE

- *Learn what leadership means.* You've already started. Getting started is always the first step, but so often people forget the first step and try to leap ahead. This first step is very simple: understand what leadership is. Study the difference between leadership and management. Really understand it and be able to articulate it to yourself and others. This understanding is your touchstone: it helps you to be sure in your role as a leader that what you're doing is genuinely what a leader should be doing. A rapid perusal of Course 1 should already have provided you with a high-level view of what leadership is and how it differs from management. You may also, by now, have a clearer understanding of your own comfort level in behaving as a manager or a leader or both.

- *Be honest and open with yourself.* It is the easiest thing in the world to fool yourself. Leaders do not walk away from the tough questions – and that includes looking at themselves. If you look hard and honestly at yourself as you get into each of the courses that follow, you will start to pinpoint those aspects of leadership that you may find really easy and those that are much harder. This is the only way to develop. Keep doing this.

- *Concentrate on behaviour.* This is what you can change. And it will rapidly have an impact on others. Moreover, as you start to change your behaviour, so you will start to feel greater confidence, certainty and boldness. Psychologists have demonstrated that, contrary to popular perception, feelings and attitudes usually follow behaviour – not the other way round. If you behave with confidence, you will start to feel more confident.

- *Monitor your leadership behaviour.* Course 7 sets out the dominant patterns or sub-domains of leadership. Once you have studied your own behaviour as a leader, you will be able to pinpoint which of the sub-domains best describes you. Then, as you review each course, use a simple process of monitoring or tracking your behaviour, in the following way:

  - What should I do more of?

  - What should I start doing?

  - What should I stop doing?

For each course (ie, each area of the leadership domain), make the list and make it simple – in short, your top priorities, not a huge list that you will never tackle. Then count (literally, *count*) how often you use this kind of behaviour. This is a technique frequently used by behavioural psychologists to help people to a) focus on behaviour (the things you can change), and b) increase or decrease the appropriate behaviour.

- *Focus first on your strengths.* Once you know where your leadership strengths lie, focus your development efforts there first. The way to make rapid impact as a leader is to a) know your strengths, and then b) *use* them. Initially, don't worry that you may not be good at some things or be uncomfortable with others. Concentrating first, or spending all or even most of your energy, on what you think of as your 'weaknesses' will, to put it directly, paralyse you. Leadership is about action. Alex Trotman, Chairman, President and CEO of Ford through the 1990s, once said, 'Complacency and sitting still when I should have been moving – that's where my biggest mistakes have been made.' Build on your strengths to give yourself greater self-confidence: these are the things you know you can do.

- *Work on your weaknesses over time.* Use the Crash Course to identify your weaknesses and make plans to modify or stop whatever activities are currently inappropriate. Begin to build new behaviour over time. It's not too difficult to stop doing things. It's much harder to start new behaviour. When you first try new ways of behaving, inevitably it may be awkward, insensitive or a little rough around the edges. Most learning is like that – and leadership is no exception.

- *Try simple tricks and tips.* Each of the courses has checklists for action as well as stories, hints and tips – the tricks, if you like, of successful leaders. Use them. Don't be embarrassed. Simple things can make a big difference: changes in posture, a new way of handling something, surprising people.

- *Learn from the mistakes that leaders make.* We are all inclined to look mainly for the positive or successful and learn from that – what effective managers or leaders do well and how such actions yield positive outcomes. Certainly, there are good reasons to do this. But you can learn as much, and sometimes more, from the mistakes that leaders make: these are the lessons that teach you what to avoid, how sequences of actions can take you in the wrong direction. Quite often, leaders make these mistakes because the logical answer is assumed to be the right answer. But leadership is about difficult choices and a sense of how you want the future to play out – the logical may be the wrong choice.

- *Do it! Turn what you know into what you do.* Most people know intuitively what leadership is and respect and warm to good leaders when they work with them. So they know what leadership is... but they don't do it. This is critical:

the distinction between what you know and what you do is *everything*. In most instances it explains why some people are successful and others not. It explains why some organizations outperform others on almost any measure over sustained periods. And it explains why some people become great leaders and most do not. The Crash Course gives you information and knowledge to help you expand your intuitive understanding of leadership into a more systematic knowledge: it helps you to know what leadership is. But turning what you know into what you do, day in, day out, is how you will become a great leader.

course **2** Impose context

Key action list and course objectives

- Provide purpose.
- Concentrate attention.
- Convey proportion.
- Avoid sending conflicting messages.
- Make rapid impact.
- Offer a future, linked to past and present.
- Say how people can contribute.
- Say what matters.
- Give clarity of focus.

As a leader you must *impose context* by concentrating people's attention on what matters in order to:

- give people a direction to take or an aspiration to pursue;

- show individuals what the key goals are;

- make sure people always have a sense of proportion and can distinguish day-to-day between what actions are important and those that are not.

MODULE 2.1: CUTTING THROUGH THE NOISE

We live in a 'noisy' world. We are everywhere assailed by information and demands for our attention – via TV, radio, mobile phones, e-mail, letters, billboard advertising – and from a huge range of people – colleagues, bosses, clients, suppliers, family, friends and so on. Many executive leaders that I have worked with frequently complain that this overwhelming avalanche of incoming data and noise means they have little or no thinking time and precious little time to relax or reflect. Employees complain that they don't know what their leaders want of them: people find it hard to know what to concentrate on, where their focus should be. This problem is made worse when people are confronted by change. 'Change?' they ask. 'But I have changed. Do I have to change again? Change to what?' Moreover, people often take their steer from the behaviour of colleagues, from the culture of an enterprise. And, despite being a leader, if you do nothing about developing the culture of the enterprise around you, it will still have a powerful influence – often in direct opposition to the behaviour you want to encourage.

So, as a leader, you are up against a bewildering array of competing voices, drawing people's attention and concentration in all sorts of directions, when what is needed is clear and focused purpose. This seems obvious, but in most instances, people get it confused or, worse, wrong. Ask yourself: do you know what matters and what does not in your business, enterprise, or work? Perhaps you do. But consider once more: if asked by one of your people, 'Does what I'm doing contribute to our objectives? Does it matter? Is it important? How does it create value?' – do you have a way to answer? If not, you need to. Also, bear in mind that very few people will ask you those questions. People don't make it easy for leaders. They usually just get on with doing things, but things that often make only a marginal or, in some cases, no contribution at all to the success of the enterprise. All the more reason for you to make sure that people have the answers to such unspoken questions.

UNCOMFORTABLE LEADERSHIP LESSON NO. 2.
A SURPRISE OF THE WORST KIND

Departmental Manager George has had bad news from head office. The business must reduce costs and improve speed of response right across the organization. George has been told to deliver a target of 15 per cent cost savings within two months. After he recovers from his initial dismay he begins to think pragmatically. He can achieve this in a number of ways – better purchasing (squeezing suppliers, and so on) – but, now he has checked the numbers yet again, he knows that people costs are one of the biggest items. There's no getting away from it. He will have to make some of his people's jobs redundant – probably three people out of his team of 50. The thought depresses him: in the year he's been their manager, he has got to know everyone personally and likes them all. They like him.

This feels like the hardest decision he's ever had to make. As he agonizes over the problem, an insistent voice at the back of his mind keeps telling him that when he announces the loss of jobs (and people) it is going to cause major disruption. The answer that presents itself time and time again as he turns it over in his mind is that he should leave any announcement until the end of the two-month deadline. 'Get all of the bad news over with at the same time,' he tells himself. So, that's what he does.

Is his decision to avoid disruption until the last possible moment a sound judgement of leadership? Will this save the business and his team from unnecessary difficulties? Are there additional consequences of this decision that he hasn't thought of?

As it turns out, rumours of the cost-cutting start to circulate. George is questioned by a couple of his team members. He denies the rumours. But three days later it is clear that he will have to say more to calm people's nerves. Hereafter, he feels that he can't keep up. Although he admits that cost-cutting is on the cards, his staff believe that wholesale redundancies are imminent. The situation has been blown out of proportion. Worse is to come: within weeks he realizes that not only is he not trusted on the cost-cutting, the distrust extends to other areas as well.

The lessons are salutary. George has failed to distinguish between a decision made for personal reasons and one made for sound reasons of leadership. He has confused these two things and has justified his personal discomfort at dealing with the forthcoming redundancies by deceiving himself that it is sensible to avoid announcing them. In terms of imposing context, he has failed to set either the current or the future context for his people (by communicating present circumstances and the change to objectives) and, worse still, has neglected to consider what the range of future consequences may be – notably, losing the trust of his team.

How am I doing?

To see how you're doing in terms of setting context, rate yourself against the behaviours shown in Table 2.1. If you're doing this for the first time, use the checklist to establish first where your strengths are and then where you need to improve. Once you've started to develop your leadership, use the checklist as a progress assessment to see how you're doing.

MODULE 2.2: KNOW YOUR ENTERPRISE!

To lead a department or a team or an entire organization, you must understand it first. You must have a genuine fact-base which reflects the true state of the organization. This doesn't mean that you have to be able to do everyone's job, or be an expert, or know more than anyone else. What it does mean is that you must find out:

- what the strengths and weaknesses of the enterprise are;
- what it has been successful at (ie where it creates value) and what it has failed in;
- who or what the enterprise serves – its purpose (see Module 2.3).

Table 2.1   *Course 2, Impose context: progress checklist*

1. I give people a clear and simple statement or story about what we're aiming to achieve here.

    Untested   Not developed   Starting to develop   Strength

2. I involve others in helping to understand the context in which we work.

    Untested   Not developed   Starting to develop   Strength

3. I collect as much information as I can (good and bad) on my enterprise, its people, competitors, and markets or customers to be able to understand the full context in which I'm leading people.

    Untested   Not developed   Starting to develop   Strength

4. I make a point of discussing with my people how they fit into the overall aims of what we want to achieve.

    Untested   Not developed   Starting to develop   Strength

5. I spend as much time communicating where we've come from and where we are now, as I do on where we're aiming to go.

    Untested   Not developed   Starting to develop   Strength

6. If I'm really uncertain about the choice between options, I push myself to make a decision as soon as possible – I never just leave it to sort itself out.

    Untested   Not developed   Starting to develop   Strength

7. If my bosses have not made it clear what our purpose and objectives are, I ask or even tell them what I think our direction should be.

    Untested   Not developed   Starting to develop   Strength

8. I use posture, gesture and tone of voice to rapidly make an impact and assert my point of view.

    Untested   Not developed   Starting to develop   Strength

These are not answers that you get once and rely upon evermore. This must be a regular review, seeking out both informal views (chats with your people, a sense of the mood of the place, outsiders' perceptions) and formal data (customer and supplier feedback, benchmark data from competitors and other enterprises). However, many leaders or aspiring leaders fall into *the trap of getting too close.*

The trap of getting too close

Some leaders end their careers early in controversy and acrimony because they have become blind to the problems of their own enterprise. John Akers and the executive team of IBM in the late 1980s fall into this camp. I have observed numerous managers at all levels who stopped looking for data on how their department really was, instead repeating the line, 'I'm very close to what's happening here. I know what's going on.' Sometimes, such leaders have simply drifted into an unquestioning acceptance of the same old sources of information or, worse still, have gradually surrounded themselves with people who modify information that should get to their leaders in raw, uncompromising form but ends up reaching them edited and distorted. The net effect is to distort leaders' understanding of the real context and to push them into the wrong decisions.

The solution to the trap of getting too close: disconnection. Being, in effect, an outsider in your own enterprise can help enormously in leading it. Since imposing context is so much about seeing the enterprise as it really is and how it should be, the capacity to stand outside a business and view it warts and all is critical. Indeed, many incoming leaders (CEOs, departmental managers, new sports coaches, even politicians taking new political office) have an extraordinary advantage in this regard, often referred to as the 'honeymoon period' or the 'first 100 days'. This is the time when you have two fantastic opportunities.

First, you are still an 'inside-outsider', to use the words of Hans Boom, a talented project manager who was responsible for the Betuwe rail construction project in The Netherlands. This means that you can get to know the enterprise in depth without suffering the constraints of being completely part of it and therefore in some way tied by its traditions, habits and culture.

Second, you have a period of time when people will treat you as an outsider and thus you can make changes an insider would have real difficulty even attempting.

HIROSHI OKUDA

One great example of a leader who was able to disconnect from management's current, short-sighted view of the enterprise is Hiroshi Okuda, Chairman and CEO of Toyota, the $115 billion car-maker. From 1995, when he became President, Okuda emphasized the need for change and constantly drew executives' attention from inside the business and their tendency to take a Japan-centric view of the world towards the global market and the future. He wanted to raise Toyota's global profile and, to make this real, pushed aggressively into the United States, Britain, France and Poland. His fellow executives credit him with both the willingness and the ability to see the bigger picture and to use this to get Toyota people to look afresh at their own enterprise, rather than relying on incremental improvements to the traditional ways of doing things.

Unfortunately, both of these opportunities erode rapidly within a few months, especially the second. You will start to be treated as 'one of us' – and of course there are advantages to that, not least winning people's trust and commitment to you. But retaining the first opportunity as an ongoing advantage is the means to avoid the 'getting too close' trap.

Sources of disconnection: how to see your enterprise as it really is

- *Customer data.* Internally sourced data is fine but much better is data-collection commissioned from third parties.

- *Consultants' reports.* This needn't be a huge consulting engagement. There are numerous small consultancies that, with the right terms of reference, can review multiple aspects of your business to provide an external, up-to-date view, for example on your strategic position versus that of competitors.

- *Benchmarking other departments or organizations.* Don't be tempted to merely benchmark against competitors – you'll learn very little from them you don't already know. Take processes or activities that are similar in organizations from various industries. Understanding the gap between what they're doing and what you're doing provides you with sources of potential innovation.

- *Staff surveys and focus groups.* Run them using an outside agency or facilitator. You'll be surprised how open employees will be and, more importantly, how many good ideas people will offer when asked.

- *The recruitment process.* If you're taking in people regularly, as most enterprises are, then you have a ready source of external data. Pre-appointment, most potential recruits are unlikely to speak their mind for fear of irritating their prospective employer, but after appointment new recruits benefit from the same advantage as a new leader (being an 'inside-outsider'). Most big consultancies like Accenture, PA, PwC, and Ernst & Young do this more or less systematically to acquire client and competitor intelligence.

- *New entrants/small niche players.* Studying how new entrants or smaller niche players do things can be instructive. The greatest threat to organizations that have tended to dominate an industry is typically from the unorthodox approaches of completely new entrants (for example Apple introducing personal computers and thereby overthrowing the hegemony of the mainframe).

MODULE 2.3: PROVIDE PURPOSE

Understanding and imposing context, as we've discussed so far, is greatly dependent on the ability of a leader to stand apart (to 'disconnect') and to have access to the right kinds of information. All of that is so much wasted effort, however, unless a leader synthesizes and extracts from the morass of data, trends, shifting market pressures, employee needs, shareholder demands, political and regulatory hurdles and technological changes the essential core of what matters to the enterprise – in short, its purpose.

Purpose is what gives our lives meaning, whether this is striving to make a million, raising children, winning Olympic gold or devoting our energies to a charitable cause. Purpose is catalytic: it galvanizes you to do something, to choose a direction, to make decisions, to act. For leadership, therefore, it is the essential step. People need a purpose and they need it communicated to them in simple terms.

UNCOMFORTABLE LEADERSHIP LESSON NO. 3. THE QUICK WIN IS SOMETIMES THE SLOW DEATH

Louise runs a large regional department. Her counterpart in Southern Region has been leading his department through a programme of changes to implement process re-engineering. Louise's region is next and she's already had offers of help from the in-house team in Southern because they have the expertise and experience. She also has the opportunity to use the same external consultants.

At their weekly management meeting, a couple of her senior managers, excited at the prospect of making the changes in record time, thereby gaining the benefits and beating the deadline, urge Louise to use some of the programme budget for temporary transfer of three people from Southern. 'Working with the consultants and with their experience,' her managers argue, 'they could not only design the changes we need here but train up our people in the new processes and procedures. We could save a helluva lot of time.' They make a persuasive case that it would be possible to beat the deadline by as much as two months.

Jane listens to everyone's views, then says, 'I like the idea of using experience from Southern to accelerate the programme here. That's a no-brainer, so we should do it.' Then she adds, 'But we need to be running not only the implementation but the bulk of the design work ourselves with our own people, rather than simply being trained by Southern and the consultants. If we can beat the deadline, good, but that's less important.'

Question: Is this a good leadership decision? Why did Louise do this?
Answer: Yes, it is a good leadership decision. Beating the deadline is a management issue: it's about efficiency. But it is much less important than gaining the commitment and ownership of Louise's department to the changes.

She knows, as every good leader does, that if people are involved, even in a small way, in creating their own context (ie designing and implementing the process changes), then they are less likely to resist the change (the 'Not Invented Here' syndrome) and more likely to make it work. The quick win, if not properly thought through, may become a longer-term slow death when the changes are covertly sabotaged or resisted by staff. From that perspective, beating the deadline will seem very short-sighted indeed.

How do I provide purpose?

Answer the following questions:

- What do I want to achieve in terms of:
    - the end state (the final destination, the overarching objective, the ultimate goal)?
    - the main way-stations along the route (destinations I have to reach before I get to the ultimate goal)?
- Why is it important? What value will it create?
- Where are we now in relation to the goal?
- Where have we come from? What has happened to get us to where we are now, both the good and the bad?
- How will I know when I've got there? What will this future destination/goal/objective look and feel like?
- Who am I leading? Who is my audience? Who do I need to engage?
- What are their expectations, if any? What are their fears?
- What might get in the way of reaching the destination?
- Who might prevent us from either starting out or getting there?
- What should my first step be?

Providing purpose might seem simple but, as you will know from observing bosses, colleagues and other leaders, few have the skills to do this effectively. Most complicate the matter. It takes practice to get through complexity and detail to simplicity and, therefore, clarity of purpose. One of the best ways to do this is to take your answers to the questions above and to construct a simple story that you can tell to anyone in your team or to a boss or to customers. Don't just think about this – that's just sloppy. *Write it down:* this gives you the discipline to structure your thoughts, to argue the logic and the appeal of the story. It will contain all the elements listed in the 10 questions above, though you may choose to emphasize some over others. But you will judge it on the basis of its clarity of focus, against the following three measures:

1. Simplicity (it will avoid complex numbers and other details).

2. Brevity (if necessary you could describe the purpose in 30 seconds).

3. Tangibility (people can understand what this objective/purpose/destination looks and feels like).

You will doubtless find that you can write down reams of information to formulate the story. That's the easy part. The discipline and the challenge is to simplify down to the essence without losing the meaning and thrust.

IBM

One of the more dramatic, but at the same time down-to-earth, examples of providing purpose is that of Lou Gerstner's early efforts at IBM, when he took on the CEO job in March 1993. He had inherited an organization in crisis, one that had crumbled from a $6 billion profit in 1990 to a $5 billion loss in 1992. Revenues were down 13 per cent. The value of its shares had collapsed. As he took the reins, it was obvious that people were clamouring for direction, a future, a vision. Gerstner told staff and the media alike:

> There has been a lot of speculation that I'm going to deliver a 'vision' of the future of IBM. The last thing IBM needs right now is a vision. What IBM needs right now is a series of very tough-minded, market-driven and highly effective strategies that deliver performance in the marketplace and shareholder value.

He then proceeded to do just that. What is most interesting about this example is the simplicity of purpose it neatly encapsulates. Gerstner was emphasizing 'performance in the marketplace' because that was precisely what IBM needed to do. It was short-term, it focused on the *now*, it hammered the point about performance but it was outward looking – on the market, at customers, the key focus that IBMers had forgotten. It was not navel-gazing, narrowly and exclusively targeted at cost-reduction. Speculating about some long-term future for IBM, although people were demanding it, was not relevant when the organization was bleeding to death. Gerstner could see that and had the courage to stand by his judgement. A year later, analysts were still seeking a vision and Gerstner still would not oblige. He only returned to the 'vision issue' in 1995 when the transformation of the company had progressed to a point where he believed it made sense to start getting employees to think more deliberately about the future, stating:

it's with an enormous sense of irony that now, almost three years later, I say this: What IBM needs most right now is a vision... IBM will lead the transition to network-centric computing by:

- continuing to create the advanced products and technologies needed to make powerful networks real; and

- working with our customers to help them fully exploit these networks.

It is important, as a leader, not to get too hung up on faddish expectations such as having a 'vision', or a 'mission'. These things are fine but people's expectations about what a vision or a mission should look like can impede your effectiveness as a leader. Most visions and missions are remote statements, full of corporate-speak, that do not connect with people's desire for purpose. Concentrate on purpose and on communicating that purpose. If the world changes, don't be afraid to change the purpose of your work, your task, your objectives, or your enterprise. Leaders fail when they allow themselves to get stuck with an outmoded purpose.

The trap of trying to do it all yourself

Don't make the mistake of taking on the impossible role of being the sole individual with the job of creating purpose for your team. Leaders are not meant to have all the answers.

The solution: involve others. Leaders involve others in extracting the data, discussing the potential ways forward and shaping the purpose. In addition, this has the benefit of *engaging* people, in the sense that no one who is actively involved in defining their own future will resist it. On the contrary, they are likely to support it more fully, as shown in Uncomfortable Leadership Lesson No. 3 and in the story below of a CEO I worked with a few years ago.

THE IMPORTANCE OF INVOLVING OTHERS

Seeking to transform his organization, this chief executive had always been a driving manager in his career. He was impatient to make things happen and was convinced, unthinkingly, that the starting point for radically changing his organization (which was under no pressure now but would be in the not-too-distant future) was to work out the new direction by himself in some detail and then begin a process of announcing it to his executive team and the organization at large. And that is precisely what he did.

To his amazement, and despite his cajoling, anger and persuasion, he could not get people to make the changes that would fulfil this new direction. Through the grapevine he began to hear that executives and employees alike were sceptical and critical of his message. Frustrated but level-headed, he examined the problem more closely and, to his credit, he learnt (the hard way) that, because there was no pressing reason for the organization to change, he needed to involve others, to let them work with him to understand for themselves the longer-term need for change and to forge the new direction over a number of weeks. In the end, everyone in the executive team felt a strong ownership of the new vision and the transformation could proceed.

MODULE 2.4: CONVEY PROPORTION

As people, we are accustomed to beginnings and ends and we tend to construct these things in our everyday behaviour within enterprises. This is perfectly reasonable and psychologically comfortable: it means that our actions and the bundles of actions we might call tasks or roles or processes do not become so large and unwieldy that we are unable to make progress. Indeed, what leaders do is to provide beginnings and ends for their people, to say, in effect: 'When we have achieved this we will have succeeded. We start here in this way...' – thus, an end and a beginning.

The trap of celebrating victory before the war is won

The trouble with beginnings and ends is that, after hard toil, we are all inclined to reach the sunny plateau and relax. Human beings are psychologically primed in such a way that when they reach a goal their motivation reduces. That's fine if you've hit the end-goal or you have the time or leisure to take a break, but in many enterprises, particularly where market competition is fierce or the pressure for change unrelenting, this behaviour can be proble-matical. As a leader you may need people to press on to the next objective, to celebrate achievement but not relax as they sustain effort in pursuit of the next goal.

The trap of believing the war is lost after defeat in battle

This is equally dangerous and is especially prevalent during large-scale change initiatives. It is a common reaction when organizations face sudden and unex-pected difficulties – witness the problems of morale faced by Kodak in the mid-1990s as nimbler, more aggressive competitors beat it time and time again and leaders responded with new initiatives, cost-cutting and retrenchments. Sport teams react in similar ways: it is very easy to 'get into a spiral of decline' on the back of defeat, each successive defeat creating the conditions for the next. These conditions can prevail for years, in spite of the best efforts of team members. In fact, quite often the erroneous solution applied, both in sports and in business organizations, is to 'try harder', to expend more effort.

APPLYING THE WRONG SOLUTION

This was very obviously the case in one division of a large bank. The division had experienced ongoing problems of underperformance. Nothing seemed to be going right. In fact they were close to losing money. The Group CEO was demanding higher levels of performance, against target, and the Divisional Vice President, who had been charged with turning the business around, had been in post for eight months. He was starting to feel the pressure. He had been driving his top team hard, accepting no excuses, and all around it was obvious that people were working at an incredible pace. Some said that they had never worked so hard in their lives. To walk through the offices was a revelation: everyone was moving at speed. Everyone had meetings through most of the working day, and often beyond. It was common for meetings to over-run. It looked like a hive of activity. But the results weren't coming through.

I took a closer look at the top team and spent time with the Divisional VP, who had brought me in to help. He was already bitter, after only eight months in the job. He said the people in the business were poor performers, nothing like the staff he'd worked with elsewhere in the Group. He believed his executive team were untalented and resistant to change. So I went to talk to them. A clearer picture began to emerge.

When the Divisional VP had taken over, he had made the assumption that people in this part of the business were simply chronic underperformers who were used to a cosy culture because of the benign market it had served in the past. Moreover, he himself had only ever led teams where the business had been successful. He had never known failure. In this division, the problems were deeply rooted and he faced a seemingly perpetual series of failures, setbacks and poor results. His response: to come down harder each time on his executive team and his staff. He kept a diary of each executive's objectives, commitments and agreed actions, together with deadlines for all of them. When a date passed, he was immediately onto the offending executive or manager. At executive meetings he invited a wide selection of executives and managers (often up to 25) with the objective that this would facilitate communication and keep everyone informed.

The sad fact was that executives, managers and staff alike were frightened of their VP. His diary-based management made them chase only those short-term objectives that he had set; they took no initiative themselves because they feared his anger. Everyone kept frantically busy because that was what he seemed to respect and value: it didn't matter what the activity was as long as it seemed to be business-related. Trying something new was likely to be seen as frivolous and risked his wrath. Of course, no one trusted anyone, because the VP trusted no one: the safest recourse was to keep busy and take no risks.

Here we see a leader who has set the context for *activity* rather than *achievement*, not by his overt communication but by his tacit assumptions and everyday behaviour. Although his leadership approach is not extreme to start with, his assumptions (of not trusting people, of checking their every move, of demanding action rather than initiative) impose a context that starts to drive the entire business down a dead-end. The business is in a spiral of decline; each defeat seems to confirm that the war is lost and it is better to hide than to stand.

The *solution*: of course, this VP had gone too far for rapid recovery. He needed to step back, begin to build trust once more – first with his executive team, then with staff. His approach of close scrutiny, waiting for people to slip up, needed to be moderated to engender real initiative-taking rather than heads-down scrambling activity. Finally, once these aspects had been fixed, he needed to draw to a close the old ways of operating, to say:

> We are starting anew. This is our past. Although we have not performed at our best and we are under pressure, it is gone. This is where we are now. Yes, it is a difficult time. More difficulties are to come, I have no doubt. But we can achieve what we set out to achieve if we try. And this is our new purpose… this is how we shall succeed.

It takes no great leap of imagination to see that the above, rather foreshortened speech would have fallen on deaf ears with the kind of sceptical, weary and suspicious staff described in the story. There is no doubt of this. But, with the actions that preceded it – building trust, working in a more open way with the executive team, encouraging openness and initiative – the VP was able to impose a new context that worked. He emphasized that there was a bigger picture beyond the churning haste of hour-to-hour activity and pressure, that the almost overwhelming ratcheting up of what seemed like setback after setback would eventually end, and that success was in sight if everyone pulled together on a number of key thrusts. In fact, this took six months and the VP went through some traumatic re-learning of leadership to achieve it, but achieve it he did. Within one year the business was back in profit and on target.

So, conveying proportion is about three things:

1. Keep your sights fixed on the longer-term. Don't look too far ahead, but avoid the immediate and the quick fix; there is always a bigger picture and it is your job as a leader not only to see it, but also to articulate it for your followers.

2. Say what matters and what does not. If what you convey to people, unwittingly or not, confuses them and they are simultaneously under pressure (due to customer demands, work volume or public expectation), then they will invariably fall into activity that is focused on the short-term. They will look for what they have to do right now to get through this. They will seek the expedient, ie what spares them immediate discomfort, like critical scrutiny or avoiding confrontation. They will also be directionless. Why directionless? Because confusion will oblige people to make their own interpretations of direction, leading to multiple objectives and goals, all of them different and contradictory.

3. Reimpose context at once if people see defeat in a setback or celebrate victory too soon. Don't wait. As the Chairman of a large pharmaceuticals corporation once said to me: 'Communicate the essence time and time again, until you are sick of saying it. Even then, you probably haven't communicated it enough!' Most people are busy with what is in front of their face: they don't look up. Moreover, in a small team or a single part of a department, what is merely a temporary stumble for the business as a whole, can seem to those team members a complete disaster. Tell them it isn't. Repeat the context.

CADBURY SCHWEPPES

Imposing context in large organizations faced with fierce competitive pressures requires CEOs and their teams to develop strategies that must break the rules of the game – otherwise their firm becomes locked in a spiral of minor strategic and operational adjustments that can end up making all the competitors in an industry look, feel and act the same. When that happens, the firm becomes undifferentiated, customers may as well buy someone else's product as yours, your profitability comes under sustained downward pressure and the intrinsic value of the company is dramatically reduced.

Cadbury Schweppes' CEO John Sunderland understood this danger. For his company the challenge was immense, as it was competing with huge rivals bringing to bear global brand strategies on an enormous scale. Sunderland and his team broke the accepted 'rules' of the industry by de-emphasizing global scale in favour of regional focus. This required tough decisions, pushed through his management teams, about which markets could not deliver profitable growth and the company would have to exit. By contrast, the new context of delivering customer and shareholder value required leaders in Cadbury Schweppes to invest more heavily in distinctive brands in specific regions – such as a big push with Dr Pepper in North America.

John Sunderland and his team were able to build the market value of Cadbury Schweppes from just over $9 billion in 1995 to $18 billion by 2004. Moreover, the successful execution of the new strategic context in the company added some $8 billion in additional value over their global competitors.

MODULE 2.5: MAKE RAPID IMPACT

One of the great myths of leadership, observed in practice almost everywhere, is that leaders must be strong, charismatic individuals. We unconsciously form our assumptions about leadership from such myths, reinforced by the people we usually identify with leadership – Churchill, John F Kennedy, General Patton, Alexander the Great – and then expect ourselves to behave accordingly in our own leadership roles. Certainly we can learn from these great leaders, but we can just as easily depress ourselves with the impossible goal of trying to be leaders in their image. It is undoubtedly true that charismatic people gain attention and can be great leaders, but charisma itself – that peculiar quality of power, of always being noticed, of filling a room with your presence – is not a prerequisite of leadership. In any event, it is exceedingly difficult to learn charisma or create the conditions around you to cultivate it.

What is important for effective leadership, however, is the skill of making rapid impact. This is something that all leaders need, especially as the world in which people work becomes more networked, linked by teams that form, interact, recombine and then quickly disband once their objective has been attained, or where people across geographies need to operate successfully together with only minimal eyeball-to-eyeball time, and, finally, where speed is not only a pressure but becomes a source of competitive advantage. In this world, a leader *must* be able to make rapid impact.

How do you make rapid impact? You do this in two ways: first, through body language – use of posture, gesture and voice. Second, assertiveness: this is *not* confrontation or aggression but rather expressing yourself in a way that is consistent with how you feel, ie making your point and getting it noticed.

MIXED MESSAGES

Terry was a senior manager I advised over a number of months. He was a reserved, introverted man who had risen in the organization because of his technical knowledge and his ability to get on with people. He was widely regarded as 'a nice guy'. Together with the automatic positional authority he got from holding a senior management role, he was able to be quite successful. Then he took on a new role with a remit to transform a department. There were numerous tough decisions to take, people had to be fired, teams had to be built, discipline injected. Terry could do all this and was respected by his staff, despite the necessity of reducing the workforce, but his impact with his own management team was poor. Although he could communicate well, he always let himself down in difficult situations (often unconsciously) and particularly when these involved dissent and confrontation.

At management team meetings, even though he was chairing, the tough managers around the table frequently disagreed with each other or argued against necessary initiatives, usually to defend the status quo in their own sub-teams. On these occasions Terry would listen to their points and, in an attempt to make progress yet keep people on side, begin to adopt a placatory, somewhat uncertain tone. Also, most important of all, even when he was being forceful in word and insisting on a particular action, his physical posture would shift. His head would drop slightly to the side, he would lean on both arms (thus getting lower to the table) and start to put his hand up to his chin and mouth. He was unable to see this, but of course others did and they read it as uncertainty, hesitation, perhaps even fear. In effect, the content of Terry's words was insisting on one thing while his posture, gesture and voice insisted that he lacked the leadership authority to make it so. This was having a serious impact on his effectiveness, that of the management team and the transformation programme.

Assertiveness and body language

These things are learnt. Failure to speak your mind or insist on a course of action is learnt over time as we grow up. Habitually using inappropriate posture, gesture and tone of voice can become so ingrained that we hardly notice it. But just as all of this can be learnt, so it can be *unlearnt* and more positive behaviour built. The behaviour shown by Terry in the case above was a mixture of inappropriate non-verbal behaviour (body language) and lack of assertiveness when dealing with members of his management team. There are four actions to take to build high-impact, assertive leadership behaviour.

First, track your current behaviour. Gaining awareness of your own behaviour through self-observation is the best way to start to change. But be specific: think carefully about how you behave in situations where you need to have impact, like management team meetings, speeches to staff or social events. Think about where you are already aware that you feel shaky, tense, nervous and regret not saying something, or where you feel disappointed with yourself but justify your behaviour by telling yourself, 'Well, I don't want to upset people. It'll work out all right; they know what I want' or, 'I'll tackle her straight-on next time.' Which specific situations are these? What is common about them? Who is present? Is it in groups rather than one-to-one?

Become aware of your body language. How does your physical posture change? Do you, like Terry in the story above, slump, sit back, lower your head? What gestures do you use? Are they normally big, expansive and expressive but become smaller, tighter, stiff and constrained? What about your tone of voice? Is it too loud or soft? Does it waver?

Second, analyse your behaviour. Gather the information described above and write it down. Analyse it by looking at the types of behaviour, posture, gesture and tone of voice you display in particular situations. *Get specific.* You will not learn to have leadership impact by generalized goals such as, 'I must be stronger and more direct.' Human beings learn behaviour in specific contexts and then adapt that behaviour to other, varying contexts. Once you have listed the *specific* behaviours, postures and gestures you need to improve, create another list next to these of the specific behaviours, postures and gestures that you want to display. Some examples are shown in Table 2.2.

Continue to track your behaviour over time, allowing yourself the luxury of feeling good about successful change but spending most of your time isolating problem areas and trying new approaches.

Third, learn high-impact behaviour in bite-sized chunks. Once you have your list of behaviours, it's tempting to try everything all at once or to look at the list and think that it's a wish list that will never be achieved. Do neither. Tackle single areas at a time, for example, those involving particular individuals in a specific situation. Look for models of the appropriate behaviour you want to learn in colleagues or other leaders you admire. Again, be *specific.* Look at the individual actions, postures and gestures they use. Then plan how to tackle the situation, rehearse the behaviour alone (looking in a mirror is useful) and finally try out the new behaviour gradually in live situations.

Fourth, get feedback on your new behaviour. A spouse, friend or mentor can help in learning leadership impact. Get them to observe you in action tackling specific situations, even if these are rehearsals. Ask them for comments on the gestures you employ, the way you sit or stand, the language you use, your tone of voice. Of course, the best feedback will come from the success you achieve in the areas you have targeted. Use it to refine your new behaviour until it becomes entirely comfortable.

Table 2.2   *Examples of specific behaviours, postures and gestures that need improving*

Current	Desired
• Was dissuaded by managers JS and RTP from taking action on the Phoenix initiative (and two other projects in their areas), usually in management committee meetings.	• Listen to what JS and RTP have to say, but stick to my guns in spite of their criticisms, excuses and even some apparently good reasoning. I do not take no for an answer.
• Nervous when I drop by JS's office to review his team's performance each week. He is always confrontational, though polite, and usually has plenty of good excuses. I end up not pushing him hard enough; tend to accept his excuses; he's also older than me and that makes it uncomfortable… I back down and let the meeting turn into a chat. Find it difficult to meet his eye. Physically, I feel uncomfortable, sit awkwardly, shuffle my papers and listen to him too much (maybe 70 per cent of the time).	• I have the weekly meeting in my office. I am perfectly clear about where he and his team are underperforming. I look him in the eye. I talk calmly and I have a single sheet of paper in front of me. When he interrupts (as he always does), I simply repeat what I have to say, insisting that he follows through. I talk loudly and firmly. I sit forward and I sit upright, despite the temptation to sit back.
• Divisional meetings: more than 30 managers there, 20 dotted-line reporting to me; I have to give some tough messages but I deliver the messages in a hesitant way. I have to have my deck of slides and I stick to them, so the presentations are stiff and formal; always stand behind a desk.	• I have a couple of slides which I use when required as well as detailed notes but I don't refer to them. I sit on the edge of the desk sometimes or walk around. I use broad, big gestures (pointing at the screen, for example) to emphasize points and I ask people if they're clear about everything. I make a few amusing remarks.

High-impact leadership: some tips

- Use your voice to good effect. A deeper tone projects greater confidence and authority.

- Sit upright at meetings and take the most central or dominant seating position (usually the head of the table).

- Use larger gestures, hands open, arms wide. Used occasionally they command attention. (Flailing hand and arm movements also attract attention but for the opposite reason!)

- Keep your chin up: you'd be surprised how many people drop their head in a submissive way when they feel uncertain.

- Finish what you have to say if you intend to say it. This doesn't mean being aggressive and interrupting others. Use prefatory remarks like, 'Let me finish my point' and then get on with it. If you do this enough, others will learn not to interrupt.

- Say what you intend but never speak simply to get airtime. Some people feel the pressure in meetings, particularly with peers or more senior colleagues, to *say something, say anything*. As a result, they say a lot but make little impact, chiefly because they're not thinking, simply reacting. Listen to the flow of discussion but spend the time thinking about what you need to say, then make your point: it is bound to have bigger impact than passively following others' ideas.

- Keep your hands away from your face, even if you're leaning on your cheek or chin at a table. When you speak this looks as though you're unsure of your words.

- Make eye contact. One-to-one this is important if you want to be sure that people will believe what you're saying or will do what you ask. In groups, eye contact makes and retains engagement with people. Leadership is all about engaging with people, getting their attention and keeping it focused.

- Say 'Yes' and mean it. Say 'No' and mean it. Speak and act in a decisive manner when it is called for. When debate and discussion are called for, listen.

Course summary

Imposing context is about cutting through the noisy organizational world with a clear, ringing message:

1. Know your enterprise: understand its strengths and weaknesses as an inside-outsider would.

2. Provide purpose: create a powerful story to direct people's energy; make it simple, brief and tangible.

3. Convey proportion: make sure people do not lose sight of your guiding purpose; don't let them see defeat in setbacks nor final victory in short-term success.

4. Make rapid impact: learn how to adjust your gestures, posture and tone of voice to assert your leadership.

3 Make risks and take risks

Key action list and course objectives

- Focus on opportunity.
- Break with convention.
- Try things.
- Ask: 'What if…?' to create opportunities.
- Pull the plug on failing initiatives.
- Do constructive damage to the status quo.
- Escalate conflict.

As a leader you must *make risks and take risks* by understanding what opportunities exist, or can be created, and then converting them into results in order to:

- pre-empt the otherwise hidden or unexpected risks that might damage the enterprise;

- take advantage of opportunities for success in the present or future;
- create new ways of doing things that are beneficial, advantageous or profitable;
- expose yourself and your people to new situations that develop thinking and skills.

MODULE 3.1: RISK MAKING, RISK TAKING

As a leader, if you're not making mistakes you're not doing anything. In this fast-paced world – no matter what the enterprise you lead – the necessity to take risks, to make and seize opportunities, to ask questions about what needs to change and then commit to changing it, is overriding. Many senior managers in large organizations are very concerned about this. They look outside their business and they see threats from competitors, especially those using new technologies or low-cost off-shore labour, that could not have been predicted even two or three years ago. Then they look inside their organizations and they see hard-working, disciplined but, frustratingly, staid and uninspiring managers who do not know how to lead, who have never learnt how to deal with rapid change or the complexity that comes with it. When the organization needs new ideas, creativity, innovation, entrepreneurial spirit, faster speed-to-market and the ability and preparedness to break with convention, there are too few, if any, leaders to make these things happen – and all of these things depend on the leadership ability and willingness to make and take risks.

Now, the make-up and personality of some people predisposes them to more opportunistic and risk-taking behaviour. Does this mean that if you are naturally cautious you will fail to make it in the leadership stakes? Does it mean that you cannot learn to take risks? No. Some psychological research is very revealing in this regard. David McClelland, a Harvard psychologist, showed that low and high achievers behave quite differently when taking risks.

Low achievers do one of two things: 1) they minimize risk as much as possible, to the extent that they severely limit all potential options and opportunities; or 2) they take wild, irrational risks, which have a higher likelihood, therefore, of failure.

High achievers, by contrast, typically take moderate risks, but the key here is that they calculate risks against circumstances and their own abilities. As a result, leaders who achieve things are usually making careful, sometimes intuitive, calculations of risk.

So, leaders do not take wild, irrational risks based on some mysterious gut instinct. Nor are they in possession of a larger than average slice of luck that gifts them wins from most of their hunches. On the contrary, leaders have three advantages:

1. Leaders are prepared to ask 'What if...' questions that *create* risks, ie *opportunities and options*.

2. They actively *calculate* the up and down sides of the options and risks.

3. They are *willing* to take a risk, ie take the decision.

This pattern of behaviour is represented in Figure 3.1.

1. 'What if...?'

The first part of this pattern is concerned with asking 'What if...?' about the current context, thereby creating opportunity options for further consideration. Do not underestimate the importance of this stage: most people have a preference (because of their upbringing and education as well as organizational norms and rules) for limiting options rather than expanding them. *Leaders create opportunities.* And the easiest way to do this is to school yourself into constantly asking yourself the 'What if...?' question. Likewise, other types of questions become equally powerful in expanding opportunities:

- What things must I change?
- How do I change things or shut them down?
- What new things can I try and when?

I am frequently challenged by healthily sceptical managers that such an approach would bring their department and, quite probably, the organization at large

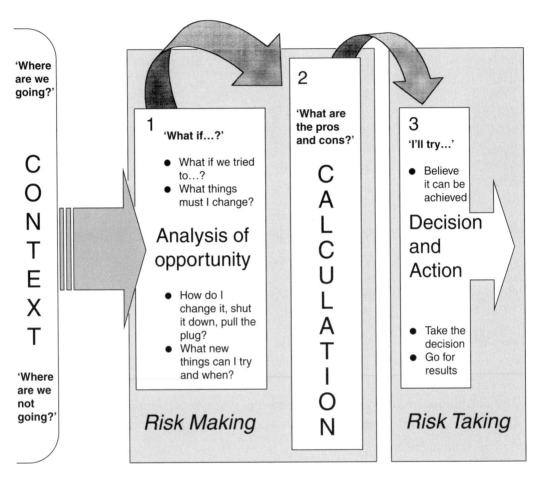

Figure 3.1   *How to make risks and take risks*

grinding to a halt. My answer is always the same: organizations are invariably so rule-bound, and the people in them so fixed into the formal and informal norms and ways of working (which are almost exclusively conservative), that you can afford 100 times the volume of 'What if…?' questions that you believe might bring the organization to a standstill. There are always going to be thousands of well-meaning and effective managers to carry out the rules and very few leaders to try to break the rules. *Leaders break rules* – it's their job. You need to do the same.

2. 'What are the pros and cons?'

The second part of the risk equation is about making some kind of calculation of the pros and cons of an opportunity – formal, data-driven, experience-based or intuitive. This is a way of getting at the potential downsides and upsides of the opportunity. Critical in achieving this will be your willingness, first, to think through the pros and cons and, second, to seek out and encourage *different* opinions and views. This *expression of difference* is very important because as you absorb the contrasting viewpoints and the extremes of potential outcomes, you gain *insight*.

PIERRE GRAVELLE

Pierre Gravelle, the deputy minister, was charged with bringing about the transformation of Revenue Canada. He engaged not only with managers and employees in challenging conventional ways of doing things, but also with external bodies such as the Canadian Bar Association, the Canadian Centre of Chartered Accountants, tax practitioner groups and industry associations. As Gravelle says, 'We were getting them to challenge us.' Moreover, when Gravelle was asked later to be CEO of Symcor, a co-sourcing venture for three of Canada's top retail banks, he drew managers together from different backgrounds, cultures and ways of working. The differences they brought to the decision-making process made things difficult at first, but those different perspectives enriched the debate and delivered insight, thereby avoiding the simple quick fix or missing real opportunities for improvements.

Some powerful ways of gaining insight are to:

- Consider the best and the worst possible outcomes, not just what you believe is the *probable* outcome.

- Exaggerate the likely threats – when you make them seem worse than they are, you frequently gain insight into how much less of a threat they really are or what the precise nature of the threat is. This frees you from fear and lack of confidence.

- Ask one of your team to play devil's advocate, that is, to always take on the role of arguing a dissenting view regarding a particular opportunity or decision. This forces you to consider alternatives.

- Take time out to consider. Don't get pressed into rapidly jumping one way or the other on risks. Insight often comes from subconscious processing of ideas, opinions and data when you're actively engaged in something completely separate from the issue or risk at hand, like going to the gym. If you feel pressured, it's much better to take the positive step of saying, 'I'm going to consider everything we've discussed and tell you my decision tomorrow.' Stick to your timescale. People will respect you for it. Delay further and you will cultivate a damaging reputation of prevarication.

3. 'I'll try it...'

Risk making is so much wasted effort if you fail to make the decision *and* take action. Thousands of good ideas, opportunities and insights go nowhere every single day in organizations because people neglect to take the step of making the decision and then taking action. If, as a result of stages 1 and 2 above, you believe there is an opportunity or the risk looks acceptable, then believe it can be achieved, demonstrate your belief by your posture, bearing and behaviour (ie project to others that you are confident) – and then take the decision.

There is one final element. Sometimes, having taken the decision, particularly one involving significant risk, leaders may sit back, forgetful for the moment that risk taking is nothing unless action follows. This requires a focus on results, making things happen, ensuring that what you decide gets implemented.

Risk checklist: what sorts of risks?

Listed below are examples of some of the sorts of risks that leaders must face, create and take. Use this list to identify areas where you may be missing opportunities or neglecting to create them, or those aspects that you need to systematically target to ensure that you are not exposed to unknown risk:

- Taking the risk of giving one of your people who is performing well an opportunity to try a bigger role earlier than he or she thinks they should.

- Taking the risk of suggesting to customers that they try a new approach outside their usual way of doing things.

- Even though things are going well, asking the question, 'What if we tackled things in a different way?'

- Knowing the target is X but taking the risk of raising people's ambition to go for X plus 10 per cent.

- Taking the risk of going to your boss to say that you have a better way of tackling things.

- Creating the risk of empowering people to come up with their own ideas and solutions to problems.

- Taking the risk of backing a fledgling initiative or new way of working that you believe has potential but is viewed by others as a waste of time.

- Taking the personal risk of presenting opposing information that will undoubtedly cause annoyance and even conflict with others.

- Sticking to your belief in following a strategy or an approach despite the risk of pressure, criticism, persuasion or even threat.

- Listening to all the arguments and options, but taking the risk of being prepared to reject all of them because they are inappropriate.

- Taking the risk of being prepared to back down and accept a better argument or option than the one you proposed.

How am I doing?

Rate yourself against the behaviours shown in Table 3.1. If you're doing this for the first time, use the checklist to establish first where your strengths are and then where you need to improve. Once you've started to develop your leadership, use the checklist as a progress assessment to see how you're doing.

Table 3.1   *Course 3, Make risks and take risks: progress checklist*

1.   I try to think 'non-traditionally', to consider new or alternative ideas as opportunities for positive change and improvement.

   | Untested | Not developed | Starting to develop | Strength |

2.   I encourage my people to suggest new ideas.

   | Untested | Not developed | Starting to develop | Strength |

3.   I take steps to protect new ideas or changes from premature and destructive criticism or actions.

   | Untested | Not developed | Starting to develop | Strength |

4.   I make sure I have access to and listen to new ideas.

   | Untested | Not developed | Starting to develop | Strength |

5.   I acknowledge mistakes (my own and others) and make the necessary changes quickly.

   | Untested | Not developed | Starting to develop | Strength |

6.   I accept that it is my job as a leader to be bold in breaking with convention when necessary.

   | Untested | Not developed | Starting to develop | Strength |

7.   If a project or initiative is plainly not working, I don't delay in pulling the plug on it.

   | Untested | Not developed | Starting to develop | Strength |

8.   When the moment comes, I don't prevaricate – I am decisive.

   | Untested | Not developed | Starting to develop | Strength |

MODULE 3.2: FOCUS ON OPPORTUNITY

Thinking about the people you work with – colleagues, bosses, your team – you will undoubtedly recognize in some of them the tendency to be sceptical, to consistently say, in response to new ideas, suggestions or changes: 'Oh, it'll never work! It can't be done… It's been tried. Might be all right in another organization, but here….' This selfsame reactionary point of view is also hidden behind comments such as, 'If it ain't broke, don't fix it.' More often than not, this is code for, 'I don't want to contemplate change.'

This is the outlook of people who are generally risk-averse. For leadership, that outlook is dangerous. *Remember that opportunities are the risks that it would be easier and safer to avoid.* Great leaders do not display risk-averse characteristics. On the contrary, they are focused on opportunity. This means having an outlook that is geared towards creating psychological space – freedom to consider alternatives and to do things differently – rather than restriction, fixed ways of behaving, tradition, convention and, critically, punishment for trying something new. This is true both of leaders themselves, ie how they think and behave, and the context or environment they cultivate for their people to inhabit.

What becomes startlingly clear when you review these two opposing outlooks is the way *control* is used. Those who are risk-averse will try to exercise complete control over people and the detail of their actions. Leaders will release control over people and their actions but retain firm control over context, ie purpose and direction. By releasing their direct control over our individual actions but within the bounds of clearly articulated purpose, leaders show us personal and collective opportunities for performing better than we believe we are capable of doing.

So this is the mindset of 'opportunity' rather than 'it can't be done'. This is where the question, 'What if…?' becomes all-important, as set out in Module 3.1. The 'What if…?' question is the simplest and most direct way to open up opportunities, on any issue. So you must ask:

- What if we were to try this new line of business?

- What if we threw out all our current, tried-and-tested tactics and started over – how would we be different?

- What if I promote Gary earlier than I might otherwise?

- What if we completely changed our procurement process?
- What if we hired people with a completely different background, age profile, education?
- What if we created an alliance with our competitors?
- What if we stopped launching products on the same day each month and varied it?

UNCOMFORTABLE LEADERSHIP LESSON NO. 4. LEADING PEOPLE IS NOT CONTROLLING PEOPLE

Ann took over as head of a large call centre. The centre had recently been organized into 'self-managed' teams with their own team leader but run, overall, strictly and tightly by the previous head. Performance was acceptable but any changes such as new ways of working, improvements in technology and so on were vigorously resisted. In fact, a situation had developed in which staff (and, more often than not, their union) regularly became embroiled with management in debating and questioning the implications of any change well beyond any constructive discussion. The new manager, Ann, had a very different philosophy, which she set out at once in her meetings with team leaders and other staff. First she listened carefully to what was being said. One of the primary themes ran like this: 'No one in management ever tells us anything...' staff would complain. 'We're kept in the dark and they don't want to know our ideas or problems.'

After a couple of weeks spent getting to grips with the operational details, Ann began to make her leadership felt. To the team leaders and the staff she spoke with, she would say two key things:

First: I hear similar concerns from most people here – that management doesn't tell you anything and doesn't listen to you. Well, I'm sitting in that office just over there with the door open and no one here comes to tell *me* anything or listen to me! We're all going to start doing that – from now. Second: I don't mind how each of the teams organizes themselves or even how they schedule each person's call coverage during shifts. You decide all that. But what I do expect and what I will judge you against are the performance criteria and targets *that I get judged against* for the whole call centre. You can work however you like within those parameters. If you hit those targets and something's going wrong, then it's my responsibility and I've undoubtedly got the targets or something else wrong – not you. If you don't hit the targets, I expect you to fix things so that you are on target and come to me for help or with suggestions if the problem is beyond your control. That's my approach. And it's simple and fair.

Ann then enumerated the performance criteria and targets. Within weeks her call centre was outperforming all other call centres in the organization and, within two months, all previous records for the business. Most notably, process and technology changes were less likely to be resisted by the teams than initiated and driven by them.

MODULE 3.3: TRY THINGS!

Probably one of the greatest obstacles a leader faces in any enterprise is where there is a pervasive culture of learnt helplessness. This typically comes about when people are confronted a number of times by stress, failures, disappointment or defeat. Quite often they have no direct control over the circumstances that led to the original failure but they start to assume, together with their colleagues, that they also have no control over other aspects of their enterprise or even their own work. Effort, they believe, makes no difference. The sense of helplessness therefore tends to hamper their performance in other stressful situations that they could in fact control. In short, they lose the motivation to respond in an effective way. Soon, fewer people in the enterprise try to effect change. The fewer people who attempt to make a difference, the less likely people generally will feel that they can affect anything in their working environment. Even worse, this behaviour makes it less likely that effective, action-oriented new joiners will stay, or even join the enterprise in the first place. Learnt helplessness has taken a vice-like and seemingly unbreakable grip.

Tips for recognizing the trap of learnt helplessness

- People show little energy or activity in the face of pressure and demands.

- Generally there is a failure to initiate action to resolve current difficulties.

- Individuals believe they cannot take action: 'There's not a lot I can do… It's out of my hands.'

- People are not encouraged by occasional successes, attributing these successes not to their own actions but to chance, luck or circumstance: 'We were lucky.'

- Individuals have low expectations of effectiveness: 'We haven't a hope. We've got about as much chance of succeeding as…'

It is when learnt helplessness is entrenched that leadership becomes so important. Two actions are called for: 1) imposing context and, in particular, conveying proportion (as set out in Course 2); and 2) trying things, and therefore demonstrating by example. In the words of one CEO, you need to show 'that every problem, every issue is resolvable… and it's up to you to do it…. Anyone, anywhere can make things happen.'

GENERAL ELECTRIC

Nowhere is this more powerfully embedded than General Electric (GE). It is one of the largest and most successful organizations in the world with sales above the $100 billion mark. Jack Welch, the legendary business leader, transformed the business during his 18 years at the helm. GE developed and trademarked a way of operating called 'work-out'. This, quite simply, is a meeting that anyone in the organization can call, at any time, to resolve a problem, streamline a process or fix an issue – without their boss present. Once the people have worked out their solution, they take it straight away to their manager who must listen and then make a decision either way – yes or no.

This is a manifestation of the overall approach to leadership in GE – informal, direct, supportive, fixing problems, taking the initiative, focused on getting things done. In other words, it's about *trying things*.

As a leader, trying things means that you must:

- Show that you are chiefly concerned with solving problems and getting things done – not avoiding tough situations or hiding from difficulties.

- Never allow a problem to simply fester, an obstacle to be left in the way or an opportunity to go begging – if you do, your people will take their steer from you.

- Take the decision, either yes or no – refusing to do so, remember, is a decision of a kind but one that has unplanned and uncontrollable consequences.

- Delegate decision-making appropriately, within clear boundaries, so that your people learn to take the initiative themselves and understand the consequences of doing so.

- Encourage people to take action, keeping you informed but not constantly waiting for permission to do anything.

- Allow people to try things and make mistakes, so long as the mistakes are truly the result of trying new things and not sloppy thinking or work, and that the lessons from the mistakes are captured and learnt.

MODULE 3.4: PULL THE PLUG

Take a hard look at your own enterprise. How many projects, initiatives, processes or activities are there that just don't add value or contribute to purpose? There are probably several you can think of immediately and, if there aren't, you're fooling yourself. Obsolete initiatives and processes persist because, more often than not, they provide a justification for someone's current daily activity. When you probe hard in these areas, you usually find people saying things like, 'It's very important. We've always done it this way.' Or they respond, 'It would cause major disruption if we changed anything – people are used to it.'

Initiative overload or project proliferation can, bizarrely, be comforting to people: the sense of action and general busyness makes them feel that progress is being made: 'Boy, I'm so busy. I'm so important!' Of course, nothing could be further from the truth. Many projects and new initiatives start as a result of trying to put things right in other earlier projects. When things don't come right, more projects are launched to bolster those that are failing or to prop up critical business activities that are not getting the support they need or expected. Worst of all, initiative overload is both a clear signal that leaders have failed to set and communicate a guiding purpose, and a constraint on achieving such purpose.

Question: How do you tell if your enterprise is suffering from project proliferation? *Answer:* Check for duplication. Two, three or more initiatives, though apparently separate, will be pursuing similar aims, resulting in massive duplication of effort and cost.

Many leaders learn the hard way that they should have examined initiatives more critically and, if they discovered them not contributing to context or purpose, have pulled the plug on them sooner. Your own role as a leader should be concerned with getting your people to ask questions about:

● why an initiative should go ahead (even if it's been running for months or years);

● what its importance is against other initiatives;

● how it fits with finances, not only this year but also one and two years from now;

● how (and this is the clincher) it contributes to overall direction or purpose.

The most incisive way to get traction as a leader and really make sure that initiatives are relevant and contribute to the enterprise is to keep dragging people back to your statement of context and purpose – the story you tell again and again (as described in Course 2). This helps to tie all activities and initiatives to an overarching focal point and thereby provides the reason why a project is no longer relevant or is off the critical path, rather than leaving a default implication that a responsible manager has failed or is somehow personally to blame. Tough action in pulling the plug on failing initiatives is hard to take (and almost impossible to sustain) if you haven't built a support framework to allow managers to terminate projects without the political fall-out of loss of face, diminished respect or permanent career damage.

Likewise, terminating failing projects quickly is essential. The longer a decision is left, the more likely supporters and sponsors of the project are to make some sort of rough fit with the legitimate agenda, producing a fatal compromise or fudge that will retard overall progress. Their action will spring from the very human need to attach value to their everyday work.

So, in summary, pulling the plug requires:

- stocktaking initiatives to check for duplication (against your overall purpose and direction);

- getting people to justify their project and why it should continue;

- building a support framework that enables managers to terminate projects without career damage (most importantly, providing a clear statement of purpose and how the project does not contribute properly to that purpose, ie an objective rather than a personal reason for termination);

- making the decision fast.

PULLING THE PLUG

A wonderful illustration of pulling the plug involved the new chief executive of a large electronics firm. In the first week of his tenure he noticed that generally in the business, managers were late for meetings, often by 20 or 30 minutes. Partly this was because people were busy, but it was also evident that this behaviour was cultural: the higher your perceived status, the more likely you were to keep others waiting. Being late was a kind of badge indicating your standing: 'I'm running late because I'm so busy and so important.'

The new CEO also knew that lateness translated directly into sloppiness with customers (internal and external) and ran right against the new culture he was determined to build to help transform the organization from a loss-maker to a success story. In his second week, therefore, he politely asked people to be on time for the next executive meeting that he was chairing and to do the same for meetings that they were running elsewhere. At the next executive meeting, set for 8 am Friday, he waited while people took their seats, then at precisely 8 am he got up and locked the boardroom doors. Four of his team of nine had not yet arrived, nor were they able to get in when they did show up.

Thereafter, once the missing executives had made their apologies, meetings behaviour improved from sloppy to perfect in a single step. More widely, this was a simple but potent signal of leadership intent to wake up the organization, starting at the very top.

MODULE 3.5: DO CONSTRUCTIVE DAMAGE TO THE STATUS QUO

It is an error frequently made by executives in trying to change their organizations, that they set out and pursue new directions, new ways of working, new processes and so on. Nothing wrong in this *per se*, but if executives strive only for the new without inflicting, as Pierre Gravelle, President of Canadian company Symcor, magnificently put it, 'constructive damage to the status quo', then they are leaving barriers that will be a drag on change and innovation.

We can put this another way. John Chisholm was the chief executive who transformed the Defence Evaluation and Research Agency from a costly and bureaucratic snail in British defence technology to a profitable, world-class tiger, later called QinetiQ. He made this point to me at the time: 'Innovation is inherently iconoclastic – it's something that breaks rules.'

Iconoclasm – the tearing down of the old, the smashing of rules, the overturning of conventional wisdom – is at least as important a set of leadership actions as those of a positive, constructive intent. Not doing constructive damage permits old ways of operating to retain their force and for people to stick to them and avoid opportunity, innovation and risk. Doing constructive damage, therefore, means forcing or triggering new, innovative behaviour at the individual level by:

● doing away with specific policies, processes or ways of working;

- changing the composition of work groups so that people from different departments or teams who would normally never interact work closely together;

- targeting benchmarks from areas or industries completely different to the conventionally accepted;

- overtly and consistently by-passing bureaucratic ways of working dominant in the culture.

Each of these tactics is aimed at triggering in people, faced with the imminent demise of many of the old ways of working, the urgency to find or create alternative, innovative solutions – critically, solutions that are not simply reiterations of the old, conventional ways of operating. Once again, this damage to the status quo should never happen in a vacuum: your crystal clear articulation of the value you are trying to create through purpose and context is what will supply the steer to your people. It will set the parameters within which they need to operate, the guidance that ensures that whatever innovations or changes they create are aligned towards the shared objectives you want them to pursue.

Doing damage to the status quo is, of course, difficult and uncomfortable for leaders. Some leaders can become so risk-averse, on the basis of a single uncomfortable experience, that they allow the experience to bleed into the culture of the enterprise.

COCA-COLA

Case in point: Coca-Cola. In 1985, the company was pushing hard to expand and to undermine its competitors, notably Pepsi, with the launch of 'New Coke', using a formula that gave the famous drink a sweeter taste, and the withdrawal of the traditional Coke. There was consumer uproar. Within a mere 77 days, Coca-Cola was forced to ditch New Coke and re-release the old style. Executives became nervous of experimentation and a culture of management conservatism began to dominate.

This was by no means a bad thing in some ways. Under the stewardship of Roberto Goizueta, who held the CEO reins for 16 years, Coca-Cola still succeeded in penetrating many markets round the world and its share price rocketed during that period by some 4,000 per cent. It did this through powerful efficiency drives and a single-minded focus on its distribution network to place the drink, as its advertising suggested, 'within an arm's reach of desire'. The strangling weeds of conservatism, however, spread throughout the corporation, culminating in the appointment of Douglas Ivester. He seemed to have no new ideas to offer, was inward-looking and badly miscued on a number of occasions on the public relations front – notably his high-handed comments about a Coke health scare in Europe, where the drink was banned for a time. In two years Ivester, a 20-year veteran of Coca-Cola, resigned, and was replaced by Doug Daft, under circumstances where the corporation had experienced two of the worst years in its history. Its stock was slumping while it was losing share even in markets such as China where it had clear advantages over Pepsi.

MODULE 3.6: ESCALATE CONFLICT

Conflict exists in all human social interaction. It is widely assumed to be a bad thing. Certainly, many types of conflict involving personal hostility or disputes within and between teams about identity or values can be destructive. And yet there are greater dangers in avoiding or suppressing conflict. Managers who, worried about their reputation or fearing criticism, desist from raising contentious issues about the way processes are working or who neglect to forward to other teams, or more senior executives, unflattering or critical data, avoid, suppress or ignore conflict with potentially devastating consequences.

THE MERCEDES A-CLASS

The A-class 'Baby Benz' was designed by Mercedes-Benz engineers under pressure to get a high-quality car to market rapidly and at a competitive price, thereby making inroads into the critical mid-size and small car market. The problems with the car were attributable to a widespread failure within middle management ranks at Mercedes Benz to raise concerns about its design and engineering. Unpalatable evidence was avoided and ignored when it should have been brought into the open and actively debated with senior management. No corrective action was taken and the car spectacularly failed a routine slalom avoidance manoeuvre called 'the Elk Test', set up to simulate avoiding hazards, like elks, on Swedish roads. The failure, unbelievably, only came to light in the full glare of media coverage when Swedish journalists from *Teknikens Varld* magazine test drove the vehicle and attempted the Elk Test. The 'Baby Benz' tipped onto its side. A car sharing the brand heritage of its larger, luxury stablemates as 'the best engineered cars in the world' had failed in the worst possible way.

After some initial defensiveness and a coordinated damage limitation exercise, Mercedes Benz acted quickly to fix the engineering problems. It also investigated, in the words of senior executives, 'why bad news didn't travel as well as good news within the business' – in other words, why difficult, contentious issues had not been passed through to executive levels where corrective action could be taken.

Escalating conflict would have prevented the Baby Benz launch debacle. But… escalate conflict? It sounds weird.

Futile, destructive, unsatisfactory – these are the epithets used to describe conflict by both managers and management writers. It is hard to find anyone who actively encourages the use of conflict. In fact, the implicit and explicit determination of most people is to identify, manage and smooth out conflict. Some organizations even offer training courses in conflict management, on the strength of a widespread belief that managing and obliterating conflict will produce positive morale and improved performance. As received wisdom it sounds convincing, but it isn't true.

Question: What is conflict?
Answer: I define it as active, often contentious dispute, debate or disagreement, typically triggered or accompanied by the presentation of contrary or opposing information.

Now, let's catalogue some of the benefits (uncovered in much recent psychological research) that can be gained from judicious escalation of conflict:

- motivation and energy to deal with underlying problems;
- making hidden or underlying issues explicit and therefore amenable to being tackled;
- sharpening people's understanding of goals (clearing up miscommunication and misunderstanding);
- stimulating individuals to define where they stand, thereby building mutual understanding between different groups;
- driving a sense of urgency;
- discouraging avoidance behaviour (such as pretending a problem doesn't exist or that everything is OK when it really isn't);
- preventing premature solutions, which achieve only half-cocked, impoverished or unintended results.

Clearly, these are all benefits that leaders would like. And, indeed, it is easy to think of intractable problems – for example, poor integration of different business units that are supposed to be working seamlessly together to service customers – that need dramatic action to flush out dysfunctional and entrenched processes, ways of working and behaviour. Unfortunately, the notion of conflict escalation is counterintuitive. It doesn't seem to make sense. Deliberately stimulating conflict is aversive for us, in the short-term at least: it produces stress, might lead to resistance, additional effort, delays, awkwardness and embarrassment. These are obvious costs rather than benefits, and they're all genuine concerns. But they are *short-term concerns*. Remember, leadership must look to the longer-term – not exclusively, but predominantly.

MICROSOFT AND THE INTERNET

A good example of this is Microsoft's involvement in the internet. It seems almost impossible to believe that executives at Microsoft, now with a huge share of the web-browser market, in the mid-1990s regarded the internet as unimportant in the future business world and even as a threat to the firm. One of the reasons they could not see its potential was because it was thought that having thousands or even just hundreds of employees hooked up to the internet would enable outsiders to breach security or introduce a virus. In the mid-1990s only a handful of personal computers on Microsoft's Redmond campus near Seattle had more than an e-mail connection to the Net. Microsoft was indeed protecting itself from the internet – and all its opportunities.

Crucially, however, the firm did have leadership behaviour cultivated by Bill Gates which, in effect, escalated conflict. For a long time Gates and his executives have actively sought suggestions, critique and comment (often by e-mail). By this means views on the internet were filtering through to him, unpalatable though they were, since they ran counter to Microsoft's strategic focus. Furthermore, long before the media explosion that really raised the internet to public consciousness and accelerated its revolutionary expansion, he turned his interest and concerns into a more coherent determination to push his executives to look more closely. It would undoubtedly have been easier to avoid this kind of challenge, debate and contentious dispute in Microsoft, and to continue to focus instead on a strategy constructed around conventional Windows-based computing, but Gates pushed it, culminating in his famous 'Internet Tidal Wave' memo sent out to employees in May 1995. The resulting impact was phenomenal. From zero share of the market, Microsoft's Internet Explorer browser grabbed 57 per cent by 1998 and, with the controversial integration or 'bundling' of the browser with the Windows operating system, rose to a monopolistic 95.4 per cent by 2002! Microsoft's share has since shrunk, slipping in recent years because of fierce competition from open-source Gecko-based browsers.

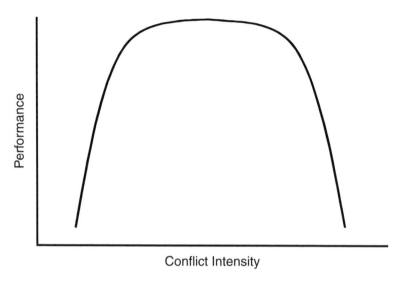

Figure 3.2   *Human performance and conflict*

The conflict curve

Another aspect of conflict that we need to understand is that at the individual level conflict can boost performance but, if escalated too much, it can create paralysis. The best way to illustrate this is to use a diagram (Figure 3.2). This shows the bell-shaped curve that psychologists use to demonstrate how human performance begins to improve as the intensity of conflict rises. However, when conflict gets too high, people become paralysed: they retreat to more rigid patterns of behaviour, they think in a more constrained way, consider fewer options or alternatives and tend to see threats when there may be none.

Task-related conflict and social conflict

Perhaps the most important thing for leaders to understand about conflict is the difference between task-related and social conflict. The key to understanding and using conflict effectively lies in mastering this distinction in practical ways. Why? Because task-related conflict typically produces desirable outcomes such as better

Table 3.2 *Task-related conflict and social conflict compared*

Task-related Conflict	Social Conflict
● Is cognitive (involving intellect, rationality, the situation and action)	● Is personalized (involving emotional interaction and relationships)
● Concerns intense debate over things such as:	● Concerns intense debate over things such as:
➢ Strategy	➢ Values
➢ Resources	➢ Norms
➢ Policies and procedures	➢ Personal identity
➢ Roles and tasks	➢ Group identity and sense of belonging
● Produces desirable outcomes such as:	● Produces undesirable outcomes such as:
➢ Better solutions	➢ Reduced performance
➢ Greater understanding of a problem	➢ Lower satisfaction
➢ Shared comprehension of complex issues	➢ Rigidity of thinking and behaviour
➢ Sense of urgency	➢ Groupthink
● Needs to be escalated (ie stimulated to an appropriate level, enouraged rather than obliterated)	● Needs to be de-escalated (ie reduced or avoided by ensuring that people agree on and are in support of common values and goals and therefore feel part of a shared group)
● Is especially important to escalate when people are under sustained time, cost and reputational pressure	● Is especially important to reduce where people are from diverse and strong national and organization cultural backgrounds (eg in global firms or after mergers and acquisitions)

solutions, greater understanding of a problem, shared comprehension of complex issues and a sense of urgency. Social conflict reduces performance and satisfaction and promotes rigidity and 'groupthink' – a tendency for everyone in a team to think in the same way and to ignore or downplay genuine threats. The differences between task-related conflict and social conflict are shown in Table 3.2.

So, the essential lesson for leaders is, first, to be alert to the real danger of peace-making initiatives where these are inappropriate (and may simply drive conflict below the surface or, worse, postpone it to a less opportune, more damaging moment) and, second, to create and exploit constructive conflict. Moreover, the best leaders make every effort to build unity and cohesion around values and norms (thus *reducing social conflict*). They will often talk about 'pulling in the same direction' and 'a single sense of purpose'.

ABB

A great exponent of this is ABB, the $40 billion global engineering corporation with some 100,000 employees in 100 countries. Percy Barnevik, the outstanding CEO who led the company from 1988 until the late 1990s, his successor Goran Lindahl, and the current CEO Fred Kindle, all have an overriding commitment to setting out, communicating, reinforcing and judging managers and employees by ABB's values. This is an active process of gluing the social fabric of the corporation together across some multiple subsidiaries and 100 countries, even during some of the recent difficulties of bringing the company back to profitability. ABB are explicit that their cultural values are responsibility, respect and determination.

How to escalate conflict: four guidelines

There are four useful guidelines to help you in the judicious use of conflict:

1. Learn to fight fairly.

2. Establish a conflict protocol as a standard throughout your team.

3. Differentiate before you integrate – express differences first before you work towards agreement.

4. Shake up the complacency of success.

1. Learn to fight fairly

It will not have escaped your notice that many of the meetings you attend, whether you work in business, government, sport or elsewhere, often deteriorate into harsh disagreement and mutual hostility, after which no business can be transacted. Recognizing that conflicts do occur and that, most of the time, it is better to prevent task-related conflict becoming social conflict, leaders need to learn to fight fairly. The four rules for fair fighting are:

- *No knock-out blows.* No one should be trying to achieve victory over others with different views.

- *Reciprocity.* Anyone in the meeting who holds opposing points of view should be allowed to make their case or argue their corner in response. Hierarchy (entrenched boss–subordinate relationships) kills this reciprocity, which is why GE's 'work-out' initially does not involve the boss.

- *Honesty.* Trying to generalize, bluff or be underhanded will also kill fair fighting. Using facts and clear evidence should be encouraged.

- *No ultimatums.* Threats are attempts at dominance and introduce the possibility either of personal attacks or a complete shutdown of task-focused debate.

2. Establish a conflict protocol as a standard throughout your team

One of your objectives in leading your team should be to communicate (if only by example) the practice of fair fighting. As a leader you have the power to legitimize constructive conflict and build it into the regularity of your team's behaviour. In pragmatic terms this means encouraging:

- an acceptance of diverse viewpoints, from the most senior to the most junior, from the most experienced to the least, valuing both internal and external perspectives;

- the examination of opposing suggestions, options or recommendations rather than simply giving them cursory attention;

- frank and intense debate;

- collaboration, sharing and speaking openly;
- the making of a sharp distinction between political manoeuvring and personal attacks (which lead to distrust and disaffection) and open, constructive conflict (which leads to task-related progress and better decisions).

3. Differentiate before you integrate

Organized social interaction (where people are organized to work together or strive for some purpose) inevitably emphasizes integration, ie early agreement or acquiescence to a decision. Such decisions are not always the best; in fact the opposite is largely true. Why? Because premature or too rapid decision-making tends to exclude material facts, data and perspectives – people are working towards decisions based on poor-quality data. As a consequence, the decisions are poor. Nevertheless, organizations, particularly in the e-world, value speed. The danger therefore is in unknowingly pushing for integration ('Let's get agreement on the way forward – fast!') before other relevant information is brought into the open, opposing interests identified or alternatives considered.

This is particularly important in strategic decision-making. Senior management must ensure that it has viable options – real alternatives based on real facts – before any strategy can be discussed or approved. Surprisingly, this leadership behaviour is very rare in most organizations.

The responsibility of leadership, therefore, is to get the sequence right. Express differences and options first, then work towards integration and decisions.

4. Shake up the complacency of success

We've talked a lot about many of the problems that organizations face and the corresponding need to escalate conflict to drive out pertinent data or opposing interests in order to make better decisions or resolve intractable difficulties. Sometimes, however, a leader becomes aware of the hidden, longer-term dangers of the *complacency of success*.

MOLSON BREWERIES

This happened to Molson Breweries, the Canadian beer giant, which had for a long time occupied the number one slot with 46 per cent market share. But in the mid-1990s it became clear to the leadership of the company that on current performance trends, their chief competitor, Labatt, already at 44 per cent share, would overtake them before the new millennium. Disseminating around the executive team a chart showing this performance trend over the coming two years was a wake-up call to everyone. It signalled a shift and stirred people out of the workaday rituals embedded in an organization where it was always assumed Molson was number one.

A number of tactics can be used to shake up complacency:

- Move managers or adjust the composition of the team.
- Raise standards or objectives, thereby driving urgency.
- Create competition between teams.
- Create contention around specific facts (as in the Molson example), processes or ways of working, then invite teams to make improvements.
- Bring in consultants to uncover and suggest changes.
- Ask team members to write their career obituary from the perspective of 10 or 15 years hence, when they retire, as a way of getting them to re-energize themselves and be clear about their personal objectives and contribution to the enterprise.

Course summary

Risk making, risk taking is about creating and seizing opportunities, asking questions about what needs to change and then committing to changing them:

1. Focus on opportunity by asking, 'What if…?'

2. Try things – and therefore demonstrate by example that every problem, every issue is resolvable. Anyone, anywhere can make things happen.

3. Pull the plug on projects, initiatives, processes or activities that just don't add value or contribute to purpose.

4. Do constructive damage to the status quo in order to trigger new, innovative behaviour at the individual level.

5. Escalate task-related conflict (in order to expose problems and to create urgency and better decisions and solutions) and reduce social conflict (in order to avoid damaging behaviour patterns such as 'groupthink' and personal and team hostility).

course 4

Challenge and change

Key action list and course objectives

- Be adventurous.
- Grab people's attention.
- Jolt your people, from time to time, out of accepting things as they are.
- Take competitors by surprise.
- Give up the past to operate in the future.

As a leader you must *challenge and change things* by experimenting and being adventurous in order to:

- grab people's attention;
- energize your followers;
- take competitors by surprise;

- jolt your people, from time to time, out of accepting things as they are, to prevent the ordinary becoming all that they believe is possible.

MODULE 4.1: UNPREDICTABILITY

There was a single human force that first drove the Industrial Revolution in Britain in the 1700s, that fired American entrepreneurs through the 1900s, fuelled the huge growth in Japan and other Asian countries in the post-World War II decades, and that in the late 20th century accelerated the pace of global technological and social change to a staggering new level we now call e-speed. This force was *inventiveness* – a willingness to go beyond the norm, to move outside the pattern and do things that are different and could not be predicted in a world that seems overwhelmingly to value the logical, the rational, the uniform, the predictable.

It is very easy in many enterprises for people to become fearful, apathetic, cynical, sceptical, stuck in a rut, or simply trapped in the workaday grind of the status quo. This is a difficulty for would-be leaders at most times, but is especially fraught when the enterprise is facing large-scale, radical change. You will have heard the comments, perhaps even been moved to utter them yourself: 'It's been done before. It'll never work. It can't be done.' So what is a leader to do when faced with such a mountain of granite scepticism or indifference? The answer: do something different. Be unpredictable. Do what no one expects. Surprise people. Ask your people to challenge you and change the way things are done. Blow them out of their ruts. *Challenge and change.*

A note of caution to the unwary and wildly enthusiastic: this is *not* a prescription for mad, gibbering actions or an excuse for irresponsible, tyrannical behaviour; it *is* a prescription for personal creativity, organizational innovation, experimentation and simply being different enough that you grab attention and stand out. If you like, challenge and change is about being somewhat rebellious, articulating and offering alternatives to the status quo – encouraging yourself and your people to go beyond the ordinary.

Table 4.1   *Course 4, Challenge and change: progress checklist*

1. I raise people's ambition by setting out new challenges and higher goals – by creating adventure.

    Untested | Not developed | Starting to develop | Strength

2. I make 'leaps ahead' – considering options or possibilities that are radically different to what is current or acceptable today.

    Untested | Not developed | Starting to develop | Strength

3. I do not allow the past (traditions, history, convention) to be a drag or obstacle in building the future.

    Untested | Not developed | Starting to develop | Strength

4. I look for new ways to energize and excite my people – to get their attention and keep it focused on our purpose.

    Untested | Not developed | Starting to develop | Strength

5. I am constantly asking my people to come up with new ways of better serving our customers, gaining an advantage over our competitors or opening up new markets.

    Untested | Not developed | Starting to develop | Strength

6. I deliberately challenge ingrained habits and rituals that sap creativity and interest in work.

    Untested | Not developed | Starting to develop | Strength

7. I encourage people to experiment, to be different and counterintuitive, to challenge each other.

    Untested | Not developed | Starting to develop | Strength

8. I drive myself to amaze my team, our customers and our markets.

    Untested | Not developed | Starting to develop | Strength

How am I doing?

Rate yourself against the behaviours shown in Table 4.1. If you are doing this for the first time, use the checklist to establish first where your strengths are and then where you need to improve. Once you've started to develop your leadership, use the checklist as a progress assessment to see how you're doing.

MODULE 4.2: CREATE ADVENTURE

It's possible that you think of the leadership challenge you have taken on, in whatever form that takes, as a difficult problem to be solved, a job to be done, a role to be filled, or a stepping stone to something better. These are all legitimate human adaptations to new circumstances, especially in the world of work. The challenge can seem daunting, each of its component demands difficult tasks that need to be completed, on time, on budget, to a standard, to precise expectations. It may excite you, this challenge. But you may still treat it as a task.

Leaders, however, self-evidently have followers. And followers will take their steer from their leader. Forgive me for hammering this point, but it goes to show that if you treat the leadership challenge as a task, so your people will treat their involvement in the purpose you have set as a mere task too. They will do their task, possibly to the standard required, but no more. They will surely fall short of their potential in developing new skills and they will certainly fail to bring to bear their creativity in improving the way things work, in engaging with customers and retaining *their* interest and loyalty.

Leaders create adventure. They invest an enterprise with excitement. They take the ordinary and make it extraordinary. They transform both the routine and the insurmountable into an undertaking with all the risks and promises that galvanize human beings to do *more*. And they do this through two main actions: they use or create threats or impending disasters, and they elevate ambition.

Leaders use or create threats or impending disasters

If there are no threats or impending disasters, leaders create them. Threats and impending disasters trigger motivation and action in the same way as primitive survival imperatives – for example, 'If we don't change, we'll be dead in the water' or, 'Corporation Z.com is stealing our market – what are we going to do about it?' or, 'There are no alternatives – we have to fight to win', and so on. This catalyst can be used at an organizational or team level to pull individuals into joining in the adventure.

Its advantage is that it helps people endorse and act upon change because the need is compelling – there are no good reasons not to follow your lead. Moreover, the bigger the threat, the bolder can be the action or the solution. This approach works very well, therefore, when the challenge is wholesale transformation of a department or an enterprise.

The problem with this tactic is that it is essentially negative and reactive. It implies a threat to which you must respond rather than proactively leading the market and the competition. In addition, it is hard for leaders to sustain their people's effort when the prime motivator is one of danger – individuals become weary and negative themselves and, over time, may abandon hope. So it is important to use this approach over the short or medium term. Finally, if the threat is real but distant, it requires leaders to materialize the threat by raising the stakes – in effect, reaching into the future to drag the threat close enough to cast its shadow over people. What helps here is painting the possible future in vivid terms: 'Our costs are running above our revenues… stock price collapse… relegation to the minor league… losing the respect of our customers… bankruptcy in two years.' Leaders therefore weave this compelling picture into the *context they impose* and use it to focus people's attention on the overriding purpose, which is quite often responding to difficult or radical change such as cost-cutting, the implementation of new technology or processes, a merger, recovering from consistently poor performance or the threat of a take-over.

Leaders elevate ambition

The second way that leaders create adventure and galvanize people into purposeful action is by giving them an ongoing sense that their everyday work is something much more than the ordinary, that it contributes directly to a great undertaking, of which it is a privilege to be a part. This is the aspiration of the 'just war' fought by Britain and the United States and their allies during World War II, or NASA's putting a human being on the Moon in 1969, or finding a cure for

AIDS. But such aspirations are not necessarily or exclusively confined to the critical milestones of world history – these are simply some of the largest and most notable of ambitions, given weight by their social importance or their impact.

Adventure can be created by any leader in most circumstances. And it need not be a one-off; it can be sustained across thousands of people in a complex multinational organization.

RICHARD BRANSON

The sense of adventure imparted by Richard Branson, the entrepreneurial CEO of the Virgin Group, is a wonderful case in point. Branson himself is the Virgin brand. He is famous for his daring high-altitude balloon adventures, attempting on a number of occasions (finally unsuccessfully) to be the first to circumnavigate the globe in a balloon. He founded and runs a sprawling enterprise from London with businesses as diverse as his airline, a passenger rail service, the Megastore retail chain, mobile phones and financial services. He also bid to run Britain's National Lottery.

In the 1980s, long before it became fashionable to see senior business executives from the dot.com internet start-ups dressing down in jeans and T-shirts, Branson was famous for his colourful sweaters. He encourages informality and discourages conformity, with the express purpose in mind that people in the Virgin Group should feel that they can have fun and be creative, taking risks on business ideas that will make Virgin's new ventures compelling propositions for customers.

His charismatic unpredictability has been a constant thorn in the side of British Airways, whose dominance and business practices he has repeatedly challenged, both in the market and in the courts. The little guy against the big guy is a role he relishes and, of course, this draws adventurous people to want to work for the organization. Here is an ambition that makes a job at Virgin so much more than just a job. At his airline, Virgin Atlantic, for example, there is no shortage of young men and women desperate to become aircrew, even though Virgin's pay packages are by no means top dollar. Joining Virgin Atlantic is not merely about the excitement of seeing the world or working for a high-performance, innovative airline; it's also about taking on and trying to beat Goliath – ie British Airways.

It's important to remember that the raw businesses that Virgin runs are no different to a hundred others – airlines, trains, financial services, retail stores. There are plenty of utterly dull organizations doing these things. What makes Virgin different and the Virgin brand so powerful is how Branson communicates, positions and values the work in his businesses – it is exciting, it is aimed at doing things that are unexpected, being better than the dominant competitor, having fun, taking part in an adventure.

UNCOMFORTABLE LEADERSHIP LESSON NO. 5. DON'T LET THE ADVENTURE BECOME ALL-CONSUMING

Robert Haas, who in 1984 became the CEO of Levi Strauss & Co, the $7 billion worldwide jeans clothing company, transformed a private (and, at the time, ailing) corporation by emphasizing its aspirations statement, conceived in 1987. This put front and centre the values of diversity, teamwork, trust, openness, ethics, recognition and empowerment. For a short while they remained just that – aspirations – until 1989 when training courses were introduced to embed the values and, most importantly, the appraisal and compensation systems were re-worked to reinforce them. Within Levi's the values were sacrosanct. People behaved in accordance with them and the corporation attracted people to work there because the values were lived. For a decade Levi's was a runaway success and grew enormously in its overseas markets, where eventually profits were some two-thirds of the corporate total.

Things ultimately went wrong for Robert Haas in the late 1990s as overheads in the US business ballooned out of control and he was accused in the business media of fatally damaging the mighty Levi's brand. Inevitably the company's commitment to its values became a casualty too as executives were forced to axe thousands of jobs. It is undoubtedly the case that most Levi's managers and employees had come to regard strict adherence to the values as more important than running a profitable enterprise. At the time, insiders commented that simple management decisions were held up interminably by wrangling, not with business-relevant issues but over convoluted interpretations of whether such decisions ran counter to the values.

Bob Haas became Chairman in 1999 and handed the CEO role to Phil Marineau, who had his hands full through to 2005 trying to reverse eight straight years of slumping sales.

The lesson for leaders is not that aspirations can be damaging. On the contrary; in Levi's case, the aspirational values were hugely important in energizing the workforce. Where Haas and his fellow leaders went wrong was in allowing the context to shift in their hands, to permit managers and staff to reinterpret the context of the enterprise by over-emphasizing consensus and strict compliance with embedded values at the expense of sensible business acumen.

MODULE 4.3: TAKE THE ORGANIZATION BY SURPRISE

Leaders who try to do the unconventional and the non-traditional and, in so doing, supersede or nullify current strengths for new advantages, will always beat their conservative peers who tend to stick to what they know. There is a difference in mindset between these two types of person. On the one hand, most people think of the elements of their enterprise – assets, systems, processes, even people – as pretty well fixed. These are the things you find around you and, beyond the odd tweak or adjustment, such people believe there is not much you can do to alter the elements or the impact that they have. On the other hand, a smaller group of people think of these elements as dynamic capabilities that not only afford power to make things happen but also must be constantly improved. Leaders do not regard this improvement or doing what is unconventional as some kind of project with a limited term. This is not a once-and-for-all push that will transform the enterprise. All elements of an enterprise need refreshing at some point – even the values or the way values are lived in an organization, as Robert Haas and his executives at Levi's discovered.

Consequently, even as the critical mass of people in your team or your organization at large become comfortable with the way things operate, the success they have achieved or, sometimes, their *inability* to make any difference, so you must disturb this sense of comfort, break up the equilibrium and call forth new endeavour.

ROLLS-ROYCE REINVENTED

Rolls-Royce is a 100-year-old global company, taking $11 billion in revenue, with 35,000 employees servicing customers in 150 countries – and it does *not* make luxury cars. Since they bought the asset in 1998, Rolls-Royce cars have been made by German carmaker BMW. Instead, Rolls-Royce designs and makes jet engines, gas-turbine generators and marine power systems. In the 1980s only a few airlines used its engines; by 2005 some 42 of the top 50 civil airlines were powered by Rolls-Royce engines. This success belies some of the difficulties the company has faced, many of them down to a heritage and consequent culture that put overwhelming emphasis on wonderful engineering. Resources and investment were steered towards research and development (R&D). This meant that the engineers rather than marketers, sales people or those running businesses had the upper hand.

When John Rose became CEO in 1996, he began to shake things up internally. While recognizing the engineering heritage and the importance of continuing to pump investment into R&D (some $4.5 billion over five years to 2006), he began to challenge the engineering mindset, which was too internally focused. He realized the company needed to direct its energies much more towards the global marketplace. The organization was streamlined into four market-oriented businesses – civil aerospace, defence aerospace, marine and, lastly, energy. Moreover, by shaking up the dominant culture from one that enthused about engineering design towards one that also valued commercial thinking, managers began to spot opportunities for stable, annuity revenues. For example, Rolls-Royce cut prices aggressively on engines in order to drive up sales. This meant a higher number of customers who require substantial aftermarket products and services, in other words spare parts and ongoing engine servicing – and where gross margins are much better than are possible through simply selling the finished engine.

This all-encompassing shake-up in the Rolls-Royce culture (and its success in driving up profitability and shareholder returns) has been achieved through John Rose's explicit strategy, outlined below:

- address four global markets;

- invest in technology, capability and infrastructure;

- develop a competitive portfolio of products and services;

- grow market share and installed product base;

- capture substantial aftermarket opportunities.

If you are unable to radically alter the organizational structure or even the physical layout of your enterprise, one straightforward way to surprise people is to break up hierarchies or boundaries but simultaneously ensure that individuals' performance objectives are tightly linked to accountability and responsibility. This may require you at times to bypass what your people expect to be 'correct channels' – like appointing a non-conformist as project leader instead of the most senior person in a team. Likewise, you can break up both boundaries and narrowly defined, constraining jobs by assembling multidisciplinary teams. In short, any combination of team that is different to the standard is a good way to disturb the equilibrium and thereby release human and organizational energy.

It follows, too, that your philosophy in rearranging teams should take advantage of making people and teams responsible for *performance* rather than for a role or a job. Instead of saying, 'Your job is to…', say, 'Your performance objectives are to…'. If you accept and reinforce narrow job definitions, then people will use them as bunkers from which to defend their narrow, rigidly defined behaviour. Your task as a leader is to bust rigid definitions that restrict performance and human potential.

Furthermore, when performance requires cross-stream working, change the way you reward people. If you have only limited control over people's pay, get a powerful grip on those aspects of reward you do control. These include praise, public commendations, a note of thanks, influence over promotion decisions, token rewards such as a bottle of champagne and, most especially in generating innovation, helping people to see their ideas brought to fruition. Quite often, achieving this last point requires leaders simply to get out of the way, or make sure the organizational bureaucracy is out of the way.

In addition, you can take the organization by surprise by deliberately moving people within the enterprise. This is not to advocate a willy-nilly whirlwind of job changing. But the careful choice of different people, with different skill-sets, to take on existing roles, can be rejuvenating for the individuals and the team. Many organizations have instituted staff job rotation or cross-business moves for managers. These efforts help in building new skills and assessing potential, but when such approaches become institutionalized in the sense that there is auto- matic and expected job movement, anticipated by all concerned, and an indi- vidual's next move is choreographed months in advance, then the whole endeavour has become predictable. In this instance, make some radical shifts:

- Persuade people to take on unexpected roles.

- Tear up the succession plan and move a maverick into a key role.

- Deliberately put off-the-wall thinkers into roles where the work pace seems to be comfortable and routine.

- Appoint energetic risk-takers to roles that span departments that must work together.

At the personal level, displaying emotion can be a distinguishing feature of leaders. One CEO I got to know was, at times, explosive and emotional, storming into fellow executives' offices and arguing through some issue or other. Mostly he was calm and well regarded, though he set very high standards. And it was when these standards were compromised that he displayed fierce emotion. People were not fearful of him and it would be totally untrue to say that he led by fear. On the contrary, he invested much time and effort in building trust with and among his executives and employees. But when he was angry, he knew the value of not with- holding the emotion. Two useful consequences emerged from this behaviour. First, the shock value of his anger created undoubted urgency and directed energy to critical areas that required immediate attention. Second, by disturbing the equilibrium, he learnt new things about his team and the particular situation –

how people would react, the extent to which they would compromise or stick to their guns, how water-tight an argument was.

Peter Ellwood, Chairman of ICI and successor to Sir Brian Pitman, CEO of Lloyds TSB, one of the most consistently successful banks in the world, has throughout his leadership career always asked tough questions of managers, getting down to the heart of the issue. This doesn't get personal: it is not an attack on an individual's analysis or efforts; it sticks to the issue or the task (as discussed in Module 3.6 under 'Task-related conflict and social conflict'). But its effect, as Ellwood points out, is that 'it makes people re-think assumptions and pre-empts complacency'. The important factor here is not to make the mistake of doing the thinking for your team; that will suck responsibility for thinking things through away from responsible managers. The tactic should be one of challenge and critique, extending the perimeters of analysis and pushing into new areas so that assumptions and complacency are driven out.

In summary, taking the organization by surprise requires you to do the following:

- Think of all the elements of your enterprise, not as fixed assets, but as dynamic capabilities that not only afford power to make things happen but also must be constantly improved.

- Alter the physical setting by regularly changing basic elements of layout, colour, furnishings and fittings. Let people decorate their own office space and take a hand yourself in overturning the ritual and habit of your people by transforming their working environment.

- Break up hierarchies or boundaries by occasionally bypassing 'accepted channels', changing the composition of teams or assembling multidisciplinary teams.

- Instead of accepting narrow job definitions and therefore 'narrow', defensive behaviour, say to your people, 'Your performance objectives are to…', rather than, 'Your job is to…', and then reward people accordingly.

- Persuade people to take on unexpected roles, appoint off-the-wall thinkers to a few key positions to create the ferment for change or new energy.

- Get angry and show it now and again.

MODULE 4.4: PROMOTE THE HERETICS

GENERAL ELECTRIC AND SEARS ROEBUCK

In the last year or so of the 1990s, GE started to identify and appoint e-business mavericks to every business. This was not some corporate think-tank holed up in GE's headquarters in Fairfield, Conn. This was people on the ground in each business, reporting at executive level, whose job was to challenge the old way of doing things and move to an e-commerce or e-business view of the world. They were actively encouraged and empowered to tear up the rule book on how GE conducts business and runs its operations. For Jack Welch, in his final year as CEO of the corporation, this was one of the most important means of grappling with both the opportunities and the turbulence that e-business would bring.

Similarly, when Arthur Martinez took over as CEO of the giant retailer Sears Roebuck & Co, he promoted and supported executives who had languished under the previous leadership because of their non-conformist views or what were considered crazy ideas that ran against the grain of the Sears culture. He got rid of most of the senior executives and, to the amazement of the old guard, appointed non-retail specialists who, because they knew next to nothing about retail, would think about the market and the business that Sears was in from completely different viewpoints and with none of the ingrained habits and prejudices of dyed-in-the-wool Sears managers. He knew he had to do this.

Arrogant, out of touch with its customer base and under severe pressure from discount-chain Wal-Mart, the once venerable Sears had lost a mammoth $3.9 billion in 1992 and Martinez had fired 50,000 people. In rebuilding, Martinez wanted to transform the company and would have no sacred cows – he was challenging and, through his appointment of the heretics, they were challenging the very traditions of the company and the market that Sears focused on and how it was served. As the thinking of the heretics evolved, so the old Sears business logic of the 'catalogue and big stores' went out of the window to be replaced with a new retail model. Like Disney, this was based on the power of singular consumer brands like Craftsman, DieHard, Weatherbeater and Kenmore delivered to middle-income families via new, small, free-standing outlets rather than just through big traditional Sears stores and big shopping malls.

This can be very uncomfortable for other executives who grew up under the old way of doing things. But then, that is the point: creating points of abrasion, new ideas rubbing against old notions, out of which come new ways of organizing, thinking and doing things. Heretics on their own are usually isolated, at best regarded with amusement and at worst as enemies or traitors. However, with your leadership support and sponsorship they become allies in jolting the larger body of people out of scepticism or a rut, challenging the status quo and moving outside the pattern. That helps you to grab attention when people in the enterprise are tending to view things from only one particular outmoded or restricted perspective.

Another leadership tactic is to cultivate a stronger current of heresy throughout the enterprise. Southwest Airlines embodies this spirit and takes it to its limits.

SOUTHWEST AIRLINES

Herb Kelleher, who co-founded Southwest Airlines in 1968 with his friend Rollin King and built it to become the $6.5 billion 30,000-person outfit it is now, is something of a heretic and maverick himself. What he has ingrained in the culture of Southwest is an excitement about being better than competitors and being different. The organization hires people who are different and places serious weight on the sense of humour that potential recruits might bring to the firm. This is not marketing hype. They genuinely want people who are outgoing, like being with other people and think for themselves. Recruitment is carefully directed to achieving this. Certainly technical proficiency and expertise are important criteria – especially for pilots! – but flamboyance, sociability and humour will swing a hiring decision. Thus, directly through their employment policy and practices they are building a culture of zany people who are not only prepared to have fun in making the passenger experience a wonderful one – especially when external problems create delays or difficulties for their customers – but also to challenge and take imaginative decisions about how to provide what they refer to in Southwest as 'positively outrageous service'.

Herb Kelleher's leadership philosophy at Southwest puts difference, imagination and fun – ie all the positive aspects of challenge and change – at the heart of his enterprise. He has achieved this in large part by hiring people in that mould and by powerful charismatic leadership to build and embed a winning *esprit de corps*.

In many organizations heretics are few and far between, or have been driven out altogether. And it is when an organization is stuck but needs to change, when the old ingrained culture is still all-powerful, that appointing a few heretics in key positions will never be enough. A leader has to build grassroots heresy, where a critical mass of people start to question the way things are done and are prepared to take the difficult first step of actually making small changes to their own behaviour or to processes and systems. One executive, faced with continuing difficulties in getting a sufficient impetus behind change in an organization that had seen multiple half-hearted efforts to improve performance founder on the rocks of resistance and scepticism, finally got his message across. He used every opportunity in interacting with employees, either one-to-one, in broadcast communications or in speeches, to say, 'I invite you to challenge authority. If you do, I will support you.' What he was doing was legitimizing heretical behaviour. There were no immediate takers. But when one or two took the risk, with the executive's full and public support, the momentum was established.

Of course, this invitation to challenge authority must be couched within the context you have imposed. Such behaviour must drive towards fulfilment of the governing objectives of the enterprise, of your leadership purpose. Attempts to sabotage, cause chaos or simply act frivolously are clearly beyond the pale – and you need to be open and unswerving on this.

Three rules apply when promoting heresy:

1. You must publicly sanction heretics' efforts – invite the challenge and reward those who rise to it.

2. You must explicitly support heretics in a sustained way – nurture heretics by clearing obstacles and supplying resources or access to resources.

3. Make it clear you do not expect them to ask for permission. This will slow everything down and takes away the underlying motivation of heretics to break rules and be different. It's much more fruitful to work on the basis that it is better to ask for forgiveness than to ask for permission.

MODULE 4.5: MAKE LEAPS – GIVE UP THE PAST TO OPERATE IN THE FUTURE

One of the truly difficult challenges leaders face is dealing with the conundrum that what made them successful as managers will not make them successful leaders. Executives fail quite often because they are overly committed to the behaviour patterns and approaches that worked for them during their career to date and cannot change. If this is true in microcosm for the personal efficacy of leaders, it is also true in macrocosm in the way leaders deal with strategic and organizational challenges: what worked for the organization in the past is not guaranteed to work for it in the future. And yet leaders are the chief custodians of that future.

In essence, the task for leaders is to eliminate all their former frames of reference in asking, 'What's the future going to look like?' They must give up the past in order to operate in the future. And we have already identified the two ways that this must happen – the personal and the organizational.

VERNON SANKEY

Vernon Sankey was the CEO of Reckitt & Colman, which became Reckitt Benckiser, the household and pharmaceutical products company responsible for famous brands such as Disprin, Lysol and Dettol, operating in some 120 countries. Sankey had been with the company man and boy and had risen ultimately to take the CEO office at a time when the firm needed to become a global organization rather than simply a loose collection of international subsidiaries.

When he kicked off the organization's global transformation, he realized that not only were his colleagues imbued with the old culture but he himself would have to change if he were to stand any chance of success in making Reckitt a global business. The business transformation was just too different, its timeframe too pressured and its magnitude too huge an undertaking to tackle in the way he had tackled the strategic and operational issues of a thus far largely static organization. Using coaching, psychometric feedback and data on his management and leadership approach, he worked hard to change himself. He commented to me at the time: 'Changing yourself, changing your behaviour is very difficult. Before this I tended to dominate discussions, I listened poorly, didn't want to spend time on the issues behind the issue; I was in a tearing hurry and wasn't taking anyone with me...'

It's impossible to change yourself through sheer dint of willpower. All behavioural change involves some kind of interaction with the environment in which you operate. Sankey drove the change in himself at the outset not only by means of coaching and data collection for personal feedback but also by asking his executive team members to tell him directly when they thought his behaviour had not been helpful. As you can imagine, it is both a difficult message to receive as a CEO and a very daunting message to deliver for those reporting to the CEO. The first time Sankey received such feedback, he immediately bridled, close to turning on the executive who was giving the feedback, but his desire to change won out. Gritting his teeth, he listened and learnt.

The second way of giving up the past is to make deliberate strategic leaps into the future. Here you are committing to do what Ford's ex-CEO Alex Trotman referred to as 'thinking about uncharted territory'. But why do this? The reason is that making leaps of this sort creates competitive advantage (whether in time, process, service, brand or product). It also helps you anticipate future trends or create options and possibilities that others may not yet have predicted. This matters because the world – most especially a business world driven to operate at e-speed – is always changing. Enterprises compete in markets that are not static: there is a constant state of disequilibrium, driven by new technology, new entrants, new forms of organization, new ideas and, of course, new leaders. Adjusting to and, more critically, *actually creating* organizational, competitive, customer and industry changes is a prime responsibility of leaders.

Making leaps, therefore, is concerned with the creation of new opportunities, with the ability to junk conventional wisdom and destroy the enterprise's emotional investment in its past strategy, forms of organization and its reputation, to violate established practices, compete in different ways, shut down competitors' angles of attack and behave in counterintuitive, unpredictable ways. As such, this responsibility sits in support of *imposing context*. When the activity that produces leaps delivers new options or possibilities, you need to test these against your context and leadership purpose. It may not often be necessary to adjust your communication of the context to followers, but from time to time this activity will present you with possibilities that require a profound shift in purpose, strategy or direction. This is demonstrated vividly in the case studies on Sir Brian Pitman at Lloyds TSB (Course 1) and John Sunderland at Cadbury Schweppes (Course 2).

Toys 'Я' Us

Toys 'Я' Us transformed the retail industry through the introduction of a new idea – huge superstores with almost every conceivable toy available to customers under one roof and, at the same time, huge product volumes allowing them to squeeze suppliers, thereby reducing prices to customers and ushering in the phenomenon of the 'category killer'. This was an attack on the current and known world and the future.

What methods can a leader use to make leaps?

Involve others beyond yourself and even your top team

This requires you to set in place the infrastructure for managers, peers, external or non-executive directors, suppliers and individuals from other industries as well as a selection of staff to contribute their perspectives. As almost every market moves towards mass customization (products and services specifically tailored to individuals but on a mass scale), so the contributions of those who best under-stand customers, customer preferences and buying shifts become important. Employees who are far from the top of the organizational hierarchy but closest to customers and suppliers enjoy a unique advantage, still inadequately tapped by leaders. Get their views and get them directly rather than through the filters and distortions of management information channels.

Build genuine challenge into any key debate around your strategic or operational future

Having the occasional away-day with your senior team outside the office environ-ment is a good start, but be sure to use an external facilitator whose brief is to chal-lenge and provoke you and the team. Conflict escalation tactics (discussed in detail in Module 3.6) should be used to promote higher levels of critique, intellec-tual analysis and boundary pushing. Your aim is not to achieve a one-off quantum leap in strategic thinking, but to instil an ethos of strategic challenge of 'what is' and the development of strategic options – not simply a variant of what has gone before.

Broaden your competitor analysis to capture ideas from industries or fields of endeavour beyond your own

If you spend your time congratulating yourself that you know precisely what your competitors or peers in the same industry are doing, you risk catastrophic failure sooner or later. Intelligence about your competitors is useful but has declining value as each year passes. The trouble is that watching your competitors with a beady eye and then benchmarking their every activity and process, copying their innovations and trying to be just that bit better than them, merely accelerates your enterprise into looking like a carbon copy. Your enterprise starts to converge on the industry norm or average, you fail to innovate and, although you may believe you are different, the differences are minor and uncompetitive. Indeed, you are probably simply taking your firm closer to commoditization of your products or services.

Remember, competitors very seldom provide answers to your problems: they think *you* have the answers. The truth is that new entrants are becoming more common and they typically invade a commoditized industry with huge innovation advantages – because they don't share the same prejudices and fixed ways of thinking as the industry incumbents and therefore bring massive and disruptive change. New entrants from other industries by and large transform the industries they target and through their innovation advantage rapidly sweep away most of the old players. Much better to be scanning industries *beyond* your own and gaining both new ideas and an early warning.

Construct an 'as is' picture and a 'to be' picture

One of the best ways to stimulate radical thinking in yourself and among your team members is to force yourself to set out in detail, honestly and unequivocally, a picture of how your enterprise operates now – the 'as is' view – and then create a future scenario – the 'to be' picture. The trigger for this might arise from several potential drivers:

- your ambition to grow the intrinsic value of the organisation;
- the threat of new entrants to your industry;
- an aspiration to take over the number one position from a dominant competitor;
- pressure from rising costs or more demanding customers;
- a new process or the development of new technology, for example the Internet;
- the action of regulatory authorities.

A useful set of criteria for delineating the 'as is' and 'to be' pictures is one I have used with executive teams, and shown in Table 4.2. There are 11 corporate or enterprise capabilities. Under each you should paint a detailed picture. Be bold. Take some risks. The differences will show you the size of the shift you will have to make to achieve your future and will force you and others to contemplate possibilities you had not dreamed of.

Invest in knowledge

Knowledge creates ideas. Over the 20th century capital and machines were at the centre of enterprise. Now, ideas are the creators of market differentiation, service,

Table 4.2   *Criteria for delineating the 'as is' and 'to be' corporate capabilities*

Corporate Capabilities	'As is'	'To Be'
Markets		
Business Portfolio		
New Products or Services		
Structure		
Finances and Assets		
Information Systems		
Processes		
Technologies		
Management Capability		
Human Resources Practices		
Culture or Values		

product, brand and wealth. Get access to knowledge. Develop formal and informal alliances with centres of excellence – universities, research organizations, consultancies. Collaborate with individuals or enterprises that own knowledge you don't have. Use the richness of the world wide web to access and leverage information.

Making leaps and sustaining the process

If these are the methods to make leaps, how should you start off and then sustain the process? Well, this needs to happen at both levels mentioned earlier in this Module, ie at the personal and organizational level.

Commit to changing your dependence on past terms of reference and ways of doing things

This can be a bit like making a New Year's resolution – you keep it for two weeks and then give up. To make it real and lasting, write down your commitment to yourself, date it and then sign it. Give it to your spouse, a trusted friend, peer or an external adviser who can help to keep you on track.

Devise and implement feedback mechanisms

Set these up with bosses, peers and your team to give you and your team a sense of how you currently tackle strategic and leadership issues. Areas of data collection and then feedback might include:

- How do my team and I currently think about the future of this enterprise?

- Who do I involve? Me alone? Some or all members of my top team? A wider cadre of managers, employees? External advisers, non-executives, industry bodies, futurists?

- What approaches do we use? Straightforward discussion? Creativity tools? A facilitator?

- How does each one of us react to new ideas? Are we dismissive, negative, responsive, encouraging, open?

- How often do we involve people with completely different backgrounds, seniority or perspectives?

Identify the changes you want to make on the basis of the feedback you get

Write them down in behavioural terms, not as broad or generalized wishes. For example, the broad action of, 'Be more open to new ideas' should be behaviourally translated as, 'Spend two hours every week talking directly to a mix of managers and employees about their ideas for change.' This makes the aspiration measurable and therefore something you will be more likely to do.

Take action

Start trying out new ways of working and moderate them to make them more effective as you track how they're going. Get feedback from colleagues. Avoid, at all costs, treating critique as an attack.

Course summary

Challenge and change is about experimenting and being adventurous in order to grab people's attention, energize your followers, take competitors by surprise and jolt your people, from time to time, out of accepting things as they are, to prevent the ordinary becoming all that they believe is possible:

1. Create adventure by using or inventing threats or impending disasters or by elevating ambition.

2. Take the organization by surprise by disturbing the equilibrium – move people around, break up hierarchies and boundaries, regularly transform the physical setting; get angry and show it.

3. Promote heretics – invite challenge and reward it; encourage people to work on the basis that it is better to ask for forgiveness than to ask for permission.

4. Make leaps by giving up the past to operate in the future; work to create genuine options that create new value.

5 Have conviction

Key action list and course objectives

- Stand on your own; have an opinion.
- Display your conviction, be fervent.
- Build relationships and trust.
- Implement a Code of Conduct.
- Tell it like it is.
- Get a regular reality check.

As a leader you must *have deep conviction* by being fervent about the things you want to achieve in order to:

- guide your decisions;
- inspire people to follow you;

- overcome the inevitable barriers and obstacles;
- have the courage to stand your ground;
- build self-belief in your people.

MODULE 5.1: CONVICTION

Conviction is the emotional bedrock of leadership. It is what enables leaders to win people to their cause, to generate energy and self-belief in followers. No one will be willing to follow a leader unless that leader believes fervently in what he or she is doing.

The 19th-century German philosopher Friedrich Nietzsche once made the inspired observation: 'Men believe in the truth of all that is seen to be strongly believed in.' What Nietzsche was remarking upon was the astounding capacity of deep conviction (in almost anything) that, by itself, can get other people to credit it as undeniable, as a fact. Put another way, if you have depth of conviction about something and you are able to display that conviction yourself by being fervent, determined and totally resolved, then you will be capable of generating a similar belief in large numbers of people. This is what creates the motive force of collective will among a leader's followers. In that sense, it is catalytic – it is an activator, it arouses people to action.

Of course, it is up to individuals to decide upon their convictions – guided by integrity, intelligence and a sense of justice. We must remember that the overwhelming force of conviction can be used for purposes both good and ill. Witness the great tyrants of history, not least Adolf Hitler. Here was a man whose fervent beliefs and talent for displaying and communicating those beliefs moved millions of Germans (and others) to war, brutal suppression of other nations and genocide. By contrast, Mahatma Gandhi inspired both political activists and tens of millions in his native India to follow his philosophy of non-violent resistance, his deep conviction guiding the country to independence from Britain in 1947. The same is true of Martin Luther King Jr in his pursuit of the cause of African Americans and his impact on the civil rights movement in the United States. His undoubted oratorical excellence sprang from deep conviction.

On a separate point, we need look no further than politics to see some of the problems occasioned by lack of conviction. Politicians in pursuit of power or in defence of the status quo have, over succeeding decades, adopted a 'sound-bite leadership' approach, one that is driven more by a need to grab attention than to make a point born of conviction. This tendency is understandable, though hardly excusable. Faced with the risk of their message being drowned by thousands of competing voices – in the form of other politicians, sports, entertainment, as well as world events that grab the limelight – communicated by a globally and locally powerful media, leaders are inclined to let their convictions be driven by the sound-bite rather than the sound-bite be driven by their convictions. The danger, in that case, is that sound-bite leadership does no more than grab the attention of an audience for a few seconds since it has no underlying belief to drive it. In this instance, people first see through the leader's words and recognize these have no conviction behind them, then become gradually more sceptical of future pronouncements, exhortations and promises. It is a lesson for every leader.

Use of the sound-bite itself can be powerful. It is, if you like, a slogan or a symbol easily communicated among followers and associated with a leader. But it must be underpinned by real conviction, not by marketing hype in pursuit of an audience. Consider, for example, Thomas Watson Sr's motto THINK at IBM. Simplistic now, but powerful in its time. Interestingly enough, Bill Gates coined a similar phrase at Microsoft. His was 'sit and think'. By this he meant that the job of most Microsoft people was to use their 'high IQ' (another concept celebrated in the recruitment practices of the firm) to produce great code and therefore great software. The structure and environment of Microsoft's Redmond campus near Seattle is the embodiment of this sound-bite: offices for each person, wonderful views outside, natural light, small groups of employees working together to produce creative spark, an egalitarian ethos where hierarchy is minimized. Gates believed all of this was essential to get the right kind of final output.

Question: Why is personal conviction important?
Answer: Three reasons:

1. *Conviction vests leaders with authority.* You should never make the mistake of believing that authority comes automatically with seniority or title. Managers have a hierarchical authority to instruct people to carry out tasks because of the

contractual force of employment terms and conditions. So people might comply with instructions but they will never carry them out with commitment to do better, or to innovate, or to make sacrifices, particularly in times of change or in the interests of the organization, its purpose or its future. Conviction can produce these things – through its own powerful intrinsic authority.

2. *Conviction attracts energy.* The pure belief in a goal, fervently and passionately expressed, acts as a homing device for people in your team. It both attracts and directs their energy to your goal or purpose rather than diffuse or wasteful activities such as office politics. In other words, conviction draws attention towards what is important and valuable.

3. *Conviction absorbs uncertainty.* We sometimes look to leaders for confirmation of our beliefs, in religion and politics most especially, for affirmation of what we should believe. Also, in times of change and the extremes of threat and disaster, we look to them to convince us that day-to-day uncertainties and misfortunes are not overwhelming and need not divert us from the goals of real importance.

WORLDCOM: BERNIE EBBERS' CORRUPTED CONVICTION

We start this course with a cautionary tale. When conviction is misguided or corrupted, the consequences for leaders and those around them can be catastrophic.

Bernard Ebbers started his working life as a bouncer, basketball coach and milkman. In 1983 he was one of the early investors in Long Distance Discount Service, the company that later became WorldCom, and a darling of Wall Street in the 1990s as it merged with or bought dozens of rivals. Ebbers had a penchant for deal-making – brashly outbidding British Telecom for the $40 billion purchase of MCI, using his WorldCom stock as currency. He confessed, or perhaps bragged, that he had little understanding of the voice and data telecommunications industry, but he knew his company had to keep getting bigger to reap economies of scale, touching 80,000 employees by 2000. That meant more acquisitions. As a leader he attracted followers and won over supporters with his excitement for the deal and his commitment to growing WorldCom's share price. He seemed unstop-pable, a genius Deal Maker (see Course 7) with a thrilling vision of a global tele-coms company.

Unfortunately, his leadership was distorted by his overwhelming obsession with WorldCom's share price (and the benefit he would reap from his own vast share-holdings in the firm) and with doing deals. What should have been front and centre for a CEO in his position, the detail of running an effective business dedi-cated to serving its customers and subscriber growth, was marginal at best. Any conviction he held about what purpose WorldCom was committed to, was over-come by misguided self-obsession. As the dot.com bubble burst, WorldCom hit trouble.

From almost nothing, WorldCom had become the second biggest long-distance phone firm in the United States, with 20 million customers. By 2002 it had racked up debts of $41 billion. Eventually an internal audit was launched into $11 billion of discrepancies in WorldCom's accounts and in 2005 Bernie Ebbers was in court to defend himself against accusations that he engineered the fraud that saw senior WorldCom executives exaggerate revenues and file false expenses between 2000 and 2002 in order to bolster the share price. Although Ebbers argued that he knew too little about the company's accounts to have directed the fraud and blamed his former finance chief, Scott Sullivan, a Manhattan federal jury found him guilty and he was sentenced to 25 years.

'Ebbers' statements deprived investors of their money,' Judge Barbara Jones said before she pronounced his sentence. 'They might have made different deci-sions had they known the truth. It seems clear to me that Ebbers was a leader of criminal activity in this case.'

And the price of leadership corrupted by self-obsession? Total losses to share-holders since WorldCom's collapse are $180 billion.

How am I doing?

Rate yourself against the behaviours shown in Table 5.1. If you are doing this for the first time, use the checklist to establish first where your strengths are and then where you need to improve. Once you've started to develop your leadership, use the checklist as a progress assessment to see how you're doing.

Table 5.1   *Course 5, Have conviction: progress checklist*

1. I believe in myself.

    Untested | Not developed | Starting to develop | Strength

2. I have my own opinions and I make them clear to others.

    Untested | Not developed | Starting to develop | Strength

3. I am prepared to make a stand for what I believe.

    Untested | Not developed | Starting to develop | Strength

4. I tell it like it is – I am open and plain-speaking.

    Untested | Not developed | Starting to develop | Strength

5. I show people by my words, actions and demeanour that I believe in what I'm doing.

    Untested | Not developed | Starting to develop | Strength

6. I build trust with others by fulfilling my promises

    Untested | Not developed | Starting to develop | Strength

7. I face up to problems and tackle them, rather than leaving them or delegating them.

    Untested | Not developed | Starting to develop | Strength

8. I get a regular reality check to make sure that my convictions are not out of control.

    Untested | Not developed | Starting to develop | Strength

MODULE 5.2: STAND ON YOUR OWN

People expect leaders to have a point of view, to express their opinions and take a stand. This is *not* the same as having all the answers. An *expert* has all the answers. One example of this, mentioned in Module 4.4, is how GE's Jack Welch regarded the internet in the late 1990s. For some time he had been sceptical about its potential usefulness and its applicability to the business context of GE. But he was open to persuasion. He let the experts build the case and, once persuaded, showed his conversion to the cause in the way he vigorously argued the e-commerce case to GE executives and employees and got people to build the capability within the company to make it real. That is conviction and the demonstration of conviction.

There are three ways to ensure that you stand on your own:

1. Have opinions and be able to defend them.

2. Listen to contrary opinions or arguments, but if you're unconvinced, stick with your conviction.

3. Examine your thoughts and feelings.

Having opinions and being able to defend them sounds straightforward. But in the maelstrom of organizational life, particularly with the demand for rapid decision-making and the pressures of political manoeuvring from which very few organizations are immune, leaders are faced with argument and counter-argument, this choice or that, option 1 and option 2 and contingencies A to Z. It can therefore be hard to have an opinion and stand your ground.

Indeed, organizational life is full of leadership tensions, the dilemmas of choosing this option over that – for example, with limited resources do you invest in the short-term or for the long-term; do you commit capital and effort to innovation or tried and trusted products; do you emphasize what is shared and global or what is distinct and local?

LEARNING TO STAND ON YOUR OWN

One executive who was otherwise a talented leader found this particularly difficult. The result was that he hesitated and agonized over most contentious decisions. As we worked together on a wider project he explained that his approach
was to listen to everyone's views and arguments and then choose the one that he
thought was right, or most appropriate or most convincing. 'Do you form your
own views or opinions,' I asked him, 'on what decision or action to take? Or do
you tend to choose from the options presented to you?' He replied that he chose
from the options. In the course of further discussion it became clear to him that he
had no opinions of his own on most of the critical issues. He simply made a choice
from among others' opinions.

What made things worse – and resulted in his prevarication on many decisions
– was his concern about insulting or hurting the feelings of those people whose
options or opinions he went against. He began to realize that carving out his own
opinions and points of view – even if they were modifications of those presented
to him – was much more important than simply acting as an arbiter between
others' viewpoints. At last he was beginning to stand on his own and felt more
confident for it too.

Naturally, there is the opposite danger of holding fast to views and opinions
beyond their value and against all rational argument. Leaders need to remain
open to persuasion, as was GE's Jack Welch in listening to the case for e-business.
The tactics of conflict escalation outlined in Module 3.6 apply here, notably estab-
lishing a conflict protocol as a standard throughout your team, which in pragmatic terms we said meant:

- an acceptance of diverse viewpoints, from the most senior to the most junior,
  from the most experienced to the least, valuing both internal and external
  perspectives;

- the examination of opposing suggestions, options or recommendations rather
  than simply giving them cursory attention;

- provoking frank and intense debate;

- emphasizing collaboration, sharing and speaking openly;

- making a sharp distinction between political manoeuvring and personal attacks (which lead to distrust and disaffection) and open, constructive conflict (which leads to task-related progress and better decisions).

Far from weakening your leadership position or grinding down your conviction, task-related conflict of the sort described above will either sharpen conviction and sense of purpose or show you where things have changed and how you need to modify them. Don't be afraid to listen to contrary arguments or to stand your ground – these are the measure of your conviction. Of course, it's not simple. The pressure to shift from a course of action or to take a new position raises doubts. Doubts undermine action and, naturally, can be sensed by the team.

Psychological research shows that those people who are able to remain optimistic under conditions of extreme stress, danger or uncertainty are much more likely to get through the experience. It is also true that some people, because of their upbringing and early social development, are naturally more optimistic than others. Certainly such people have an advantage as leaders. Their natural optimism encourages others and provides a beacon in the darkness. Optimistic people are also distinguished by their ability to keep trying things, in spite of the odds. Instead of trying to puzzle out a grand solution to what seems an overwhelming problem – and therefore becoming frozen into immobility by the sense of impossibility that it creates – optimists will do four things:

1. Think of the danger, difficulty or uncertain situation as a problem to be solved.

2. Break the problem up into smaller component parts, rather than trying to handle the whole thing.

3. Tackle each of the component parts in turn.

4. Take action; try things.

These are behaviours. And behaviours can be learnt. You can learn to behave as an optimist. But in learning to do this you need to be able to examine your own thoughts and feelings. Instead of pretending that you are convinced, thereby prolonging your own uncertainty and, as a consequence, the wider uncertainty of your people, take the time to ask of yourself the following questions:

● Am I convinced?

● Do I believe in this?

● If I don't believe it, why not? What is missing? What makes me uncomfortable?

● How does it fit with my overall context, objectives or purpose?

● If I know what is missing or makes me uncomfortable, then what should I change and how should I change it?

But, when you have considered your thoughts and feelings, take action. Any action is better than no action. No action drives you further into uncertainty, doubt and apathy. Stand on your own and try things.

MODULE 5.3: DISPLAY YOUR CONVICTION

Your conviction is of little value to anyone other than yourself if you fail to demonstrate it to others. This means that you have to be bold, you have to show that your heart is in it. You cannot risk a disconnection between what you say and what you do or even what you say and how you say it.

RUDI

Rudi was the Vice President of a successful business unit in a large multinational organization. He was a talented strategic thinker, a tough, no-nonsense manager who got things done and was destined for bigger things, according to more senior executives. Even the CEO had a favourable opinion. She believed that Rudi's strategic abilities and intellect marked him as someone who could create substantial new business opportunities for the firm. He had already demonstrated as much.

But there were some slight issues of concern. His management style was somewhat aloof; he was known to like and support his favourites in the management team and beyond, sparing little time for those he believed were 'not on side' or were underperforming. Among his peers in the executive group people respected his undoubted talents and – if the truth be known – were a little envious of his success at an early age, but they commented to each other about his off-hand remarks and sometimes biting wit. The CEO would have been inclined to dismiss these things because they seemed minor, but when she was asked to consider Rudi for a larger role in a business unit that was growing rapidly, she realized what it was that was making her uncomfortable. Rudi lacked the ability to take people with him. As she gathered more information on his performance and leadership approach, she discovered that he would say he was supportive of people but then make some off-hand remark that undermined the intent of his words. Only those who were closest to him and had worked with him for many years understood that he was joking. Rudi himself had no idea of the effect he was having.

For example, he was asked to attend a launch meeting of a new line of business and, while he telephoned the manager responsible to say how much he supported the new line and had kept up-to-date on developments throughout the pre-launch preparations, he decided not to go to the launch itself. Eventually, word got back to him that employees believed the new line of business was unimportant and that he was dismissing it as a waste of time. He was amazed. His CEO was not. She understood the symbolic power of leadership – saying something is simply not enough; you have to demonstrate it; you have to be present; you have to show you are engaged with people and that your conviction is more than just words.

The case above shows how important it is to display your conviction. If you have particular ways of behaving – an off-hand manner or aloofness, for example – that do not match your words or your intent, then people will misread your intent. If this happens you will be associated, perhaps unfairly, with hypocrisy and expedience. This makes it harder and harder to be a leader, to take people with you and build their own self-belief.

Key actions for ensuring that you display your conviction

State your position; be bold

Never assume that people know what you believe, what your position is or what your intentions are. Say what you believe in and be prepared to defend it. The behaviours that display conviction are: *firmness* – do not waver or hesitate; and *seriousness* – conviction is no laughing matter; don't undermine it by joking about it.

Track your own behaviour and get feedback

Use a simple process of monitoring or tracking your behaviour to make sure that you are being true to your conviction. The questions you should ask take this form:

In showing my conviction or commitment to aspects of work:

● What should I do more of?

● What should I start doing?

● What should I stop doing?

Use this basic pro forma on your own but, better still, get feedback from your colleagues (bosses, peers, your team).

Match behaviour to word

Start from the assumption that whatever you say about what you believe in is pure rhetoric and needs something to reinforce it, to demonstrate that what you're saying is important, meaningful and relevant. This means:

● being around at significant events;

● taking the time to talk to people, one-to-one in the places they work;

● taking action to change things (processes, rules, regulations, roles) that run counter to or that obstruct your intent or what you have promised;

● behaving in accordance with the values you preach or support.

Recognize others who take action to live up to your conviction

Go out of your way to recognize and reward team members who are living up to the spirit of your conviction. Jack Welch did this in getting GE's e-commerce initiative launched and embedded into the company. IBM's CEO Lou Gerstner did it when trying to get executives and managers to refocus on the customer and customers' needs rather than IBM's needs and its outmoded conventions about doing business.

MODULE 5.4: BUILD RELATIONSHIPS AND TRUST

Trust is the expectancy of people that they can rely on your word as a leader. This is important in enabling your people to accept responsibility – in the same way that you are accepting leadership responsibility – as well as in getting them to sacrifice their own self-interest for the sake of the purpose or direction you have set. Trust elevates levels of commitment and sustains effort and performance without the need for management controls and close monitoring. This still means you can challenge and change things as long as the basis of your relationship with others is one of trust.

Trust is built through consistency and integrity in relationships. Its prime behavioural attributes are:

- sharing appropriate information, especially about oneself;
- willingness to be influenced;
- avoiding the abuse of team-members' vulnerability (because of their lack of positional power or inadequate access to information, and so on);
- being fair;
- fulfilling promises.

TRUST

The departmental management team of a large utility business was faced with the task of implementing a comprehensive change programme involving all processes and all employees in their department. Some of the changes would require people in new team structures to work much more closely cross-stream, to be more proactive in pursuing and responding to internal customers and raising levels of performance. The management team were committed to the change: they had each declared this in management meetings and the Department Head, Andy, had explained in no uncertain terms how important it was to make this change work.

It had become apparent within a few months, however, that the change was not really happening. Greater effort was put into trying to persuade employees to adopt the new ways of working and to accelerate the change programme to avoid lagging behind the project plan milestones. To no avail. The new operational streams seemed to be working in isolation, morale was low, complaints and absence from work were high and, to cap it all, there had been two embarrassing and high-profile mess-ups with customers. The management team were putting in longer and longer days but it was not until Andy, visiting staff at one of the sites during lunch, overheard a chance remark, that he began to realize the problem might lie in the management team itself. 'The top team are divided,' was the comment. 'They're just in it for themselves.'

Andy was annoyed by the remark, but in the car back to his office he began to reflect more deeply. It could be true. Although everyone in the management team agreed on the change and the way forward, Andy had no way of knowing what happened when the managers got back to their operational streams. In any event, he had tried everything else to fix the problem in the department. He decided to get outside help: this problem was too delicate to tackle on his own. That decision also triggered another revelation: if he felt he couldn't tackle this himself, then the degree of openness and trust in his team must be poor indeed. Puzzled but still sceptical, he got an outside consultant to run interviews with each member of the management team to get any issues out on the table.

The consultant reported back, having had a couple of sessions with each manager. She confirmed that none of the managers really trusted one another. Back in their own operational streams, they frequently counteracted, in word and in deed, what had been agreed in the management team. There were jealousies and political concerns about who was gaining advantage or who was underperforming. As a result, no one was helping anyone else. They felt they had to defend their team against the others, with minimal cooperation – the very opposite behaviour to that required by the change programme.

Andy was appalled, but with the issues out in the open he at last felt able to do something. On the consultant's advice, he fed back the results to each member of the management team. Then, in a series of away-days, they began to spend time together, not just hammering away at the business and programme requirements but on getting to know each other and developing ways of solving the issues that had been getting in the way. Within two months the level of trust had developed beyond recognition from the old days. Many of the problems that were acting as corporate treacle lower down the department quickly melted away once the top team started to work together as a *team* – that is, a group of people who trusted and relied on each other instead of competing at every level.

For Andy the lesson was a profound one. His management team had not been up to the challenge of the change programme and, indeed, it was the change programme itself that had brought to light the underlying inadequacy of the team. Furthermore, his own leadership had been found wanting. First, he had allowed a situation to arise where there was little real trust in his team; on the surface people were polite, but behind each other's backs there was minimal support and cooperation. Second, he had failed to detect the problem in his own team or had chosen to ignore the signs, concentrating instead on the 'technical' demands of business and the challenge of the change programme.

So if leadership is, incontestably, about people, then it is also about continually striving to build relationships between them – not just between a leader and his or her people, but between followers. It is not enough just to take an interest in those who like you or those whom you like and respect. Building relationships requires the building of trust. In a large enterprise, with a shifting population or team structures regularly changing, building relationships of trust is an ongoing process – too easily neglected by leaders.

In circumstances where you are new to a leadership role or you have taken on a new team, or you recognize, like Andy in the case above, that there are underlying team issues, a sequence of clear actions is needed.

How do I build trust in my enterprise?

Get to know your people

Initially, you must concentrate on your immediate team. Then you must move beyond that. Break out of the standard work-based routines of interaction where behaviour tends to be regulated by unspoken rules of engagement on what you can talk about and how you interact – work only, irrelevant social chit-chat, polite discussion, respect for hierarchy and so on. Talk to people at lunch. Arrange a regular once-a-month management team lunch or dinner. Be prepared to talk about yourself, rather than just everyday work – your interests, your background, your ambitions for the enterprise.

Get the underlying issues out

In the initial stages, get round everyone at least twice for dedicated one-to-one sessions to explore their concerns, worries about work issues, ambitions, difficulties with other team members, suggestions for improvements, etc. Show them you care about them, but not by (what will be seen as) spurious expressions of interest. Simply listen. Hear what they have to say. Do not use this as a medium for pontificating on your own plans and aspirations.

Tackle the one-to-ones yourself if you're new to the job. You benefit from the phenomenon of the 'first 100 days' in which people treat you as an objective outsider in whom they are prepared to confide information and issues normally kept hidden from bosses. This also helps in building levels of trust with you – people are sharing confidential information. But remember: treat what they say with complete confidentiality. State that you plan to use the gist of what they say anonymously in order to solve problems and make progress, but that the exact comments will go no further than you.

If circumstances are more difficult, use an outsider (a consultant or disinterested facilitator) to get under the skin of the typically fractious but hidden dynamics of team working in organizations.

Establish a conflict protocol as a standard throughout your team

The details of this are covered in Module 3.6. One of your objectives in leading your team should be to communicate (if only by example) the practice of fair fighting. When things get tough, this is the best way to develop and sustain trust. As a leader you have the power to legitimize constructive conflict and build it into the regularity of your team's behaviour, thus avoiding hidden, destructive manoeuvring and personal competition. In pragmatic terms this means encouraging:

- an acceptance of diverse viewpoints, from the most senior to the most junior, from the most experienced to the least, valuing both internal and external perspectives;

- the examination of opposing suggestions, options or recommendations rather than simply giving them cursory attention;

- provoking frank and intense debate;

- emphasizing collaboration, sharing and speaking openly;

- making a sharp distinction between political manoeuvring and personal attacks (which lead to distrust and disaffection) and open, constructive conflict (which leads to task-related progress and better decisions).

Develop and implement a Code of Conduct for your team

This is a model for the sorts of behaviour you want to see as normal and which can be observed by people lower down the organization as a model which they can respect because it sets out standards and rules about how people deal with each other.

The Code need not be explicit, but the effort of developing it *with your team* and then writing it down helps to give it real power. Some leaders base the Code on the values of the organization, *but* they always make absolutely sure that the Code is behavioural (that it can be understood in straightforward action terms) and therefore can be followed and that when it is not, offenders must face consequences. Here is an example.

CODE OF CONDUCT

- We are one team; we work together in a supportive way and take joint responsibility for each other's actions. We do not criticize behind others' backs.

- We give and accept constructive criticism. We are prepared to use conflict in a positive way – particularly where there are disputes or unresolved issues.

- We are disciplined in managing performance of ourselves and our people. We give feedback in a consistent and direct way. We are not afraid to tell people that they are underperforming and to help them to improve.

- We use time effectively. We stick to the set start and end times of meetings. If someone has not arrived, we get going without them. We always reach conclusions and take action.

- We keep people informed, communicating actively and widely to all those who need to be kept informed.

Do what you promise

There is no quicker way to destroy trust than to fail to deliver on your promises. This is where consistency is important. If you have agreed to get something done for a team member by a particular date, bust a gut to make sure you do it. Likewise, make no promises you are uncertain that you can fulfil. If you are uncertain, tell people you cannot give guarantees, rather than allowing false hopes to grow.

UNCOMFORTABLE LEADERSHIP LESSON NO. 6. HAVING UTTER CONVICTION... ABOUT YOUR OWN SELF-IMPORTANCE

Frank was a successful executive who had risen rapidly in the organization. He had started straight from school, was bright but didn't go to university. Starting at the bottom he worked hard and did very well, always fiercely supporting and staying loyal to bosses he admired. Eventually the tactic paid off and one of his old bosses got him onto an accelerated management development track. He made sure during the four-year programme that he always did the right thing, worked hard and was politically astute. In fact, he believed that the internal politics of the organization were more important than anything else in successfully climbing what he liked to call 'the greasy pole'.

Colleagues and subordinates held very mixed views about Frank. Most said they 'respected him' but probably meant that they feared him and, in the same breath, said he had strong views, was 'explosive' and 'very demanding'. It was not unknown for him to fly off the handle over what seemed to others to be trivial matters. For instance, one supervisor delivered a report an hour after a 5pm deadline: Frank sat him in his office for half an hour while he shouted and stormed at him over his 'appalling work standards'. Someone else came to a meeting without having sent papers in advance. Frank flew into a rage, berating the poor individual in front of his colleagues.

In contrast, a small group of Frank's subordinates were extremely loyal, claiming to others that they 'owed him everything' and doing their utmost to support him, often taking his side or arguing his case even when it was obvious to most people that a different decision or action was called for. A few managers had found him impossible to deal with but normally *they* ended up being the ones to back down or had no real evidence to support their claims that Frank was abusive and wasn't serving the company's best interests.

Frank's career was going well – as he never tired of telling people – and he landed several high-profile roles, tackling them in his usual aggressive, bullying style. Typically, he moved on to the next role when he had orchestrated a success or had cleverly justified problems by exaggerating the size of the challenge he faced and blaming the inadequacy of the people involved. In most interactions he talked about himself and his achievements, highlighting his successes, flattering his own skills in comparison with others and emphasizing the importance of high work standards – thereby justifying the need for toughness and directness in dealing with 'the useless people out there'.

He would never cross his bosses. Much effort went towards demonstrating to them that he was loyal and that he respected their position in the hierarchy. Most knew that he was somewhat difficult to work with, but he used charm and jokes to get round this, often being disarmingly self-deprecating to more senior executives.

In the end, however, he hit a career ceiling. His suspicious, aggressive, self-aggrandizing approach to managing began to be noticed by senior executives. Having a small loyal cadre of people around him was enough for Frank to get by and to give the impression of success, but not enough to really make a deep impact – particularly when the leadership roles got more challenging and the use of bullying only made things worse. Where he was successful he achieved things at great cost – to morale, additional resource and time frames. He usually justified these things behind clever excuses such as, 'Boy, they always give me the most difficult jobs!' or 'the lousy, intellectually stupid people that are holding us all back, with their rock-bottom standards.' Few argued with him, knowing his explosive inclinations.

A few senior executives began to take a closer look at his career and his usual approach to management. They noticed that he preferred so-called trouble-shooting roles where the department was usually making losses or dealing with intractable problems, where his bullying, self-conceited style fitted well and where any problems he himself created could be concealed behind the general difficulties. Closer examination revealed that almost no one trusted him, though they could not put their finger on the reason. He had also politically 'knifed' a wide group of colleagues on the way up, some of whom had long memories. Moreover, it was clear that he was incapable of taking more than a tiny group of loyal supporters with him in any endeavour. Inspiring people, getting them to make sacrifices for the good of colleagues or the organization or even keeping up morale were skills beyond him. Ultimately stuck and distrusted by both colleagues and senior executives, he realized that he could go no further with his ambitions in the organization. Secretly he justified his difficulties by believing that everyone in the organization had 'gone soft' and weren't prepared to take the tough decisions.

This type of leader is not uncommon. They hold strong convictions – but they are convictions about their own self-importance. Most often the self-importance, born of deep-rooted insecurities and fears developed in a difficult childhood, drives other behaviour, such as needing control over others in case their self-importance is brought into question. Bullying, aggression, the cultivation of a small loyal band of followers and the 'excommunication' of those who challenge are all characteristics of these leaders. All these characteristics, of course, are useful in helping people to make an impact in enterprises, even in getting to the very top. In the end, however, such leaders are undone because their overriding purpose is self-serving and few people, if any, will follow such a cause (see Course 7 for a full description of this type of leader – the 'Spin Doctor').

MODULE 5.5: TELL IT LIKE IT IS

The trap of not saying what you mean

Most social interaction involves us in obeying unwritten rules. This varies by national culture and again by organizational culture. For example, we tend to stick to polite modes of discussion and debate. Often we do not say what we mean, particularly when we have something difficult to communicate – we assume and in some cases hope that others will understand our drift without forcing us to be explicit.

The trap of avoiding the unpleasant or the difficult

It is perfectly natural behaviour for most of us to deal with the things we like rather than those we dislike or that we find boring. This is doubly so for difficult decisions or trying interactions. We would all much rather get on with the exciting and the enjoyable, dispatching unpleasant business to the bottom of the pile or delegating it to other people to deal with.

The trap of too many triumphs won and threats overcome

This is a trap laid for leaders in the longer term. It comes about where a leader experiences a string of successes, interrupted by substantive difficulties or challenges *but over which he or she invariably triumphs*. This pattern of experience builds and reinforces beliefs of supreme effectiveness. Nothing can stand in their way.

For a while such leaders' soaring self-confidence, almost on its own, will carry the day because people will support them unquestioningly – their leader always wins.

The problems arise when a new challenge hits the horizon which these leaders do not really understand but which they whole-heartedly believe they can overcome. Their vaulting self-confidence drives them to a blinkered, head-on clash equipped with skills and knowledge they have overestimated and against a challenge they have underestimated. Pride and self-confidence make them inclined to reject other perspectives and suggestions. They believe their way is the only way; after all, they are the supreme leader. Usually they fall in dramatic fashion because their efforts to overcome the challenge have blown the situation out of all proportion. There is nowhere to go but down.

The trap of hearing only what it suits you to hear

Leaders inevitably have information passed through to them via other people – often lots of other people, since you may rely on numerous individuals or be leading a complex enterprise. Over time you are inclined to allow to grow up around you a set way of collecting and absorbing information based on your preferences and, critically, how your people interpret your preferences. Most people will automatically oblige you in what they believe you want to hear rather than what you should be told – the salutary tale of the emperor's new clothes. It is also no surprise that they will tell you things it suits them best to tell. These information distortions eventually become hardwired into your leadership approach – and truth and accuracy become casualties.

The trap of uncompromising conviction

Conviction is only one of the elements that make up leadership. Out of balance with the others, its impact on leaders will be to encourage and entrench the autocratic and the authoritarian, to separate them from their followers or to push them towards high-risk strategies, ventures and tactics out of synchrony with the purpose of the enterprise or the needs of its members. Such leaders usually are distinguished by an aura of the 'great hero' and a corporate mythology that celebrates their greatness. These characteristics are commonly associated with entrepreneurial leaders – Henry Ford, Thomas Watson Sr at IBM, Soichiro Honda, Bill Gates at Microsoft, Steve Jobs at Apple Computer – but also political leaders such as Richard Nixon and Margaret Thatcher. Where their conviction becomes detached from reality or becomes self-serving, the problems start.

Combine all of these traps and you can see the danger for leaders:

- the unwritten rules of social interaction that encourage us to be polite rather than explicit;
- the tendency to avoid the unpleasant tasks or to delegate them;
- overestimation of your skills and knowledge in circumstances you have under-estimated;
- the natural inclination of people to tell leaders what they think they want to hear.

Distortions that you don't know about become irretrievable errors in the fabric of the enterprise you lead.

There are three essential tactics for skirting these traps:

1. Face up to problems and tackle them.
2. Tell it like it is.
3. Get a regular reality check – get others to tell you how it is.

1. Face up to problems and tackle them

Don't leave problems that are too difficult or problematic. To walk away from the uncomfortable decisions or actions causes more problems later. The same is true of taking the easy route of delegating tough problems that you know you should handle yourself. Don't fudge decisions. Get to grips with them: they usually end up being less uncomfortable than you first imagine and you will be in a minority of people who do this. That gives you a distinctive advantage and other people will both respect you for it and follow your lead.

2. Tell it like it is

Most of the time it is better to be honest and plain-speaking. Putting a gloss on a tough situation because you think people will be alarmed or frightened is not to lead people but to try to control them by controlling the information they receive. That approach is becoming less and less tenable as new technologies and e-speed make information rapidly accessible and cheap; as the workforce becomes at once more educated and more demanding; and customers' needs and expectations force enterprises to make information available and transparent at the prime point of contact. One leader in a chief executive role, talking about his experience in a large internet-related business, put it this way to me:

> Our jobs at this level and other levels in the business are so pressurized, the situation changing so fast, and the nature of our business so complex sometimes that we cannot afford to be bullshitting each other. We need to know how it is – now! Then we can make decisions fast and get on to the next thing.

He spends a good deal of his time reinforcing the culture of communicating with energy and openness – both the triumphs and disasters. The key steps here are:

- Be open and honest in your communication.
- Tell people fast, as soon as possible.
- Give them an opportunity to respond – especially to get anger and frustration out.
- Tell them the action you're going to take in moving forward.

3. Get a regular reality check

When you hold powerful convictions and you occupy a leadership position that can easily become insulated against bad news and protected from healthy challenge, you must ensure that you get a blast of cold reality from time to time. This means deliberately getting access to the bad news as well as the good – about the enterprise and about yourself. Getting a reality check depends on your willingness and ability to engage with others, both inside and outside the enterprise, who can offer you perspectives to which you normally have no access. Sources of data are:

- Your own team – via objective, perhaps anonymous feedback. All this needs is a piece of paper for each person and the instruction to get back to you with honest feedback on any aspect, troublesome, positive or otherwise.

- External or non-executive directors – and not just within statutory limits; you can treat external board directors as an irritation to be tolerated or you can use their objectivity as a valuable, even if sometimes uncomfortable, data source.

- External advisers, mentors or coaches.

- Internal mentors – for example, peers or more senior executives elsewhere in the enterprise who are prepared to listen and reflect on your situation.

- Consultants – who can be commissioned to provide an objective view of any or all aspects of your organization or your own leadership.

Course summary

Having conviction is concerned with being fervent about the things you want to achieve in order to guide your decisions, inspire people to follow you, overcome the inevitable barriers and obstacles, have the courage to stand your ground and build self-belief in your people:

1. Stand on your own – have a point of view, express your opinions and take a stand.

2. Display your conviction – be bold, state your position, be firm and show that your heart is in it.

3. Build relationships and trust by sharing information, getting the issues out and fulfilling your promises.

4. Tell it like it is by being honest and plain-speaking, facing up to problems and tackling them and getting a regular reality check.

6 Generate critical mass

Key action list and course objectives

- Use influencing behaviours.
- Get people making decisions.
- Turn knowledge into action.
- Create urgency and restlessness.
- Finish what you start.
- Build an ethos or climate of people development.

As a leader you must *generate critical mass* by influencing people and turning knowledge into action in order to:

- channel your people's energy into the appropriate activities;

- mobilize all your people to work together in a coordinated way (rather than in an individualistic, haphazard manner);

- make things happen.

MODULE 6.1: DOING MORE THAN MAKING THINGS HAPPEN

In the last Course we looked at *conviction*, and while the emotional force of leadership conviction can produce unsurpassed collective will among your people, alone it cannot move people in the direction you intend, in line with purpose and the context you impose. Conviction is a catalyst: it activates. But it is uncontrolled. Consider for a moment the sudden, huge and catalytic power of popular protests – the spontaneous upsurge of violent protest in Los Angeles following the televised broadcast of members of the LA Police Department's beating of Rodney King; the rapid collapse of Communist rule in Eastern Europe and the fall of the Berlin Wall as masses of people took to the streets; protests and clashes in London over the Conservative government's imposition of the 'Poll Tax'. These outpourings of human action are powerful but uncontrolled and unpredictable.

The emotional charge among a mass of people who come together in protest or, if you wish, as a mob, demonstrates the underlying power of conviction. Where the energy created by these convictions is more organized and reaches a sufficiently large mass of people, so its impact is greater and also more sustainable. For example, what became a global movement speaking for tens of millions of people started as a haphazard series of protests by like-minded individuals at the fringes of society. What movement is this? Greenpeace.

It is also interesting that the internet has accelerated both the local and the international power of similar protest groups, allowing them to organize simultaneously in multiple locations to project the force of their protest to a much wider audience. In 1999 movements like 'Reclaim the Streets', the 'Rainforest Action Network', student activists, militant vegetarians and others were coordinated by a loose umbrella organization calling itself Direct Action Network, their normally disparate voices brought together in protest against what they regarded as predatory exploitation by global capitalism. All of the demonstrations were timed to coincide with a World Trade Organization meeting on 30 November 1999, the simultaneous protests in Seattle and London reaching sufficient critical mass to make news bulletins in a host of countries. In fact, Seattle alone saw 50,000 people join the protest on the streets.

We observe a similar phenomenon when we examine 'charisma' or 'star attraction' or 'popularity' – the power of stars in music, film and television to attract huge followings, sometimes numbered in tens of millions. But their charisma does not create any purposeful action other than for most of the public to be more than averagely interested in the star and what he or she says and does. A smaller but no less significant proportion of people dedicate what we can only characterize as an obsessive amount of time and energy to thinking and talking about the 'star', collecting photographs, books, articles, clothes and so on and in some ways trying to be like the star. Moreover, most stars do little with this latent power. It is channelled in no particular direction and to no particular cause – except perhaps their own wealth. They are, in a sense, *latent leaders*: they have grabbed attention, they are probably higher-than-average risk-takers, they may even have deep convictions, but either they neglect to or they choose not to champion a cause or use their celebrity to make things happen on a wider stage.

One exception is Bob Geldof, former front man of the band The Boom Town Rats. On the back of his musical fame he was the driving force for Live Aid in 1985 and continued campaigning to help alleviate famine in Ethiopia. In 2005 he used his fame, conviction and connections to organize and launch the Live 8 concert in London, backed by simultaneous concerts in cities around the world, to draw attention to the G8 or Group of Eight most powerful and richest countries meeting in Scotland. His intention was to put pressure on the G8 heads of government to take action, particularly in the case of Africa, to 'make poverty history'.

DIANA, PRINCESS OF WALES

The late Diana, Princess of Wales, understood this quality and was prepared to channel the energy created by it in the latter years of her life – a life, as everyone knows, cut tragically short. The unprecedented global public interest, media coverage and voracious appetite for seeing and hearing about everything she did became a vehicle not only for her multiple charitable works (after all, many public figures have trod a similar path) but also for her moral stand on big international issues. She had great success in raising public awareness of AIDS, then in puncturing the myths surrounding the illness. She later raised the game considerably in tackling the politically troublesome issue of landmines. She played a central role, until her death in Paris in 1997, in helping to build the international public call for a ban on landmines so that the political will was triggered to do the same in law in most countries across the world.

One of the many qualities that distinguished Diana and enabled her to make such an enormous impact worldwide was the perception among hundreds of millions of people that she carried real conviction – as indeed she did. People believed her and believed in her. More important, by taking on a leadership role (which is precisely what she did, though few would have dared suggest it), she used her influence, her choice of public appearances, her patronage and simply her presence to direct the huge energies of her followers into support for the causes closest to her heart.

In small and large enterprises alike, the motive power of conviction, inspiration or interest can be quickly dissipated by multiple demands – from customers, administrators, suppliers, alliance partners and so on. It can also be dissipated by the simple lack of interest shown by leaders themselves. If they have little enthusiasm for a task, a project or a purpose, so followers will lose interest.

Moreover, traditional concepts of how you organize, manage and lead people in enterprises have started to crumble. Hierarchy, command and control, boss–subordinate reporting lines and so on are still used all over the world but have decreasing relevance. This is not to say that the rigour and discipline of management structures will become irrelevant. For many of the small, fast, innovative dot.com companies spawned in the internet fever around the new millennium, the need for rigour and discipline quickly became apparent as they gained scale and complexity. Indeed, many dot.coms went under for want of organizational rigour and financial discipline. The minority that have survived, like Amazon.com, Google, eBay, Yahoo and Lastminute.com, have successfully merged the traditional and the new. Different kinds of management structure have become relevant. In many instances the old ways of organizing have been replaced by self-managed work teams, flatter organizational structures, networks, and project teams that are formed for a specific purpose and then disbanded. But all of these things have an element in common: they are to do with the channelling of energy. From a leadership point of view, the intention in channelling this energy is not simply to produce individual action – though clearly that is important – but to create in an enterprise sufficient charge or impetus to ensure that a state of *critical behaviour mass*, involving the largest possible number of people, is reached and sustained. Generating critical mass, therefore, is concerned with making things happen and making them happen at scale. The concept of critical mass is important because it is analogous to the principle in physics, denoting that point when a change in action or characteristics occurs.

To achieve this requires leadership to have a direct impact on the behaviour of many people and involves the use of the following actions:

- influencing and persuading;
- building an agenda for action;
- creating urgency;
- clearing obstacles;
- using knowledge by turning it into action;
- encouraging learning and development;
- getting out of the way.

JEFF BEZOS: AMAZON.TOAST?

The founder of Amazon.com, Jeff Bezos, used his own and his parents' money to launch the company in 1995 with a vision that millions of people worldwide would buy books online. A couple of years later in 1997, the traditional 'bricks & mortar' bookseller, Barnes & Noble, fired back at the innovative upstart by launching their own rival website. Most observers agreed with the comment of the CEO of Forrester Research who infamously remarked that the bookseller war would result in Bezos's firm becoming 'Amazon.toast'. The same year, Amazon floated on the stock market at $18 a share and in the dot.com exuberance of 1999, its shares hit $113. Although the firm made losses of $1.4 billion in 2000 and laid off 15 per cent of its workforce, by 2003, having posted its first annual profit, the company's value was $50 billion. Toast it was certainly not.

Founder, chairman and CEO of Amazon, Bezos is undoubtedly a Visionary leader (see Course 7). He had the foresight to imagine a world where people shopped online – an utterly fanciful idea in the mid-1990s. He shrugged off difficulties and criticism – from analysts, competitors and the media, as well as his own cautious managers – to persist with risky ideas and to learn from unsuccessful initiatives, like opening the firm's website so that third-party, independent merchants could hawk their wares on Amazon.com. Irrepressibly optimistic, he made 'leaps of faith', as he puts it, to challenge and change received wisdom and open up new opportunities for the longer-term – for example by dramatically cutting prices and offering free shipping on orders of $25 or more, a decision which loses the firm millions of dollars but appeals to Bezos's deeply held conviction about the primacy of the customer. The instinct at the firm is to think and act longer-term to increase the frequency with which customers will shop with Amazon rather than elsewhere. And generally, though he values risk and experimentation, he was smart at demanding from his managers that they ground their decisions in fact and back their thinking with the numbers.

But was Jeff Bezos still the right leader for a company nearing $9 billion in sales, past the excitement of entrepreneurial lift-off? Were his leadership capabilities in generating critical mass overwhelmed by his instinct for risk and new ideas? Some investors made unfavourable comparisons with Google, Yahoo and eBay and questioned whether Bezos alone *was* Amazon and vice versa, leaving the firm lamentably short of high-quality management and therefore exposed. All three of those dot.coms, now outperforming Amazon, had replaced their founders with new leaders, equipped to take the firms to maturity and build value. Amazon seemed to be faltering and, like many entrepreneurs before him, maybe Bezos needed to hand over the reins of the firm he created to a business leader who could build the critical mass – greater depth of management and a more consistent focus on return on investment.

How am I doing?

Rate yourself against the behaviours shown in Table 6.1. If you are doing this for the first time, use the checklist to establish first where your strengths are and then where you need to improve. Once you've started to develop your leadership, use the checklist as a progress assessment to see how you're doing.

MODULE 6.2: USE INFLUENCING TACTICS

I have described leadership elsewhere in the Crash Course as getting people to do things they have never thought of doing, do not believe are possible or that they do not want to do. *Using influence is therefore essential.* It is true that many people in organizations believe that the formal authority, trappings and titles accorded those entering so-called 'leadership positions' give them automatic power to lead. That is an error of judgement, as cautioned in Module 5.1. There I remarked that while hierarchical or positional authority enables you to instruct people to carry out tasks because of the contractual force of employment terms and conditions, you will never do more than get them to *comply* with instructions. They will never carry them out with commitment to do better, nor will they innovate or make sacrifices, particularly in times of change or in the interests of the organization, its purpose or its future.

That said, leaders should be able to make use of the full range of influencing behaviour. There are times, for example, when building a coalition or consensus is the best approach to take – when you are trying to get peers or team members to buy into and support a new idea or way of working, or when you are dealing with difficult labour negotiations. By contrast, at times of crisis, leading by diktat is essential: this means decisive, uncompromising, directive leadership with little regard for either the discomfort or support of others. In other words, crisis demands leadership that gets people working in concert towards a goal as rapidly as possible. Table 6.2 sets out the basic guidelines for the range of influencing behaviours.

Table 6.1   *Course 6, Generate critical mass: progress checklist*

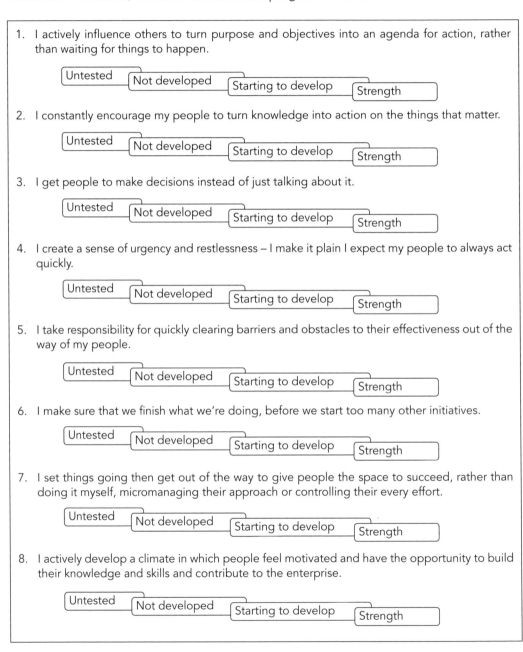

1. I actively influence others to turn purpose and objectives into an agenda for action, rather than waiting for things to happen.

    Untested   Not developed   Starting to develop   Strength

2. I constantly encourage my people to turn knowledge into action on the things that matter.

    Untested   Not developed   Starting to develop   Strength

3. I get people to make decisions instead of just talking about it.

    Untested   Not developed   Starting to develop   Strength

4. I create a sense of urgency and restlessness – I make it plain I expect my people to always act quickly.

    Untested   Not developed   Starting to develop   Strength

5. I take responsibility for quickly clearing barriers and obstacles to their effectiveness out of the way of my people.

    Untested   Not developed   Starting to develop   Strength

6. I make sure that we finish what we're doing, before we start too many other initiatives.

    Untested   Not developed   Starting to develop   Strength

7. I set things going then get out of the way to give people the space to succeed, rather than doing it myself, micromanaging their approach or controlling their every effort.

    Untested   Not developed   Starting to develop   Strength

8. I actively develop a climate in which people feel motivated and have the opportunity to build their knowledge and skills and contribute to the enterprise.

    Untested   Not developed   Starting to develop   Strength

Table 6.2   *Using the right influencing behaviour at the right times*

Type of Influence Behaviour	Most Appropriate Circumstances or Time to use the Influence Behaviour	What it Produces
1. *Ultimatums:* threat, real or implicit, that punishing consequences will follow non-compliance. 'If you don't do it, then...'	Under conditions of severe or unreasoning resistance or danger	*Compliance:* short-term and occasional tactic; if used repeatedly, requires step-wise escalation of the threat
2. *Diktat:* forceful, uncompromising directiveness; telling people how things will be and what to do. 'This is what we are going to do...'	In times of crisis; at the start of radical change; under threat of disaster	*Compliance:* in the right circumstances has a powerful, energizing effect on followers
3. *Pressure:* constant monitoring, close oversight. 'I will be constantly checking...'	Turnaround situations, especially conditions of 'learned helplessness'	*Compliance:* can be sustained over medium term but needs to be bolstered and then replaced by commitment-building tactics
4. *Transaction:* 'deal-making' exchange of 'x' in return for some specified behaviour or action. 'If you do "x", I'll do "y".'	When positions are entrenched; the relationship is highly formal or contractually constrained; or expectations are transaction-based (eg sales forces, trading floors)	*Compliance:* your influence will survive only as long as the transaction is in place
5. *Coalition building:* constructing broad front of influence, via short- or medium-term loyalty, either through sheer weight of numbers or the combined power of the constituencies. 'If we join forces, we can...'	Where existing constituencies are polarized and entrenched; when it is difficult to make headway because of vested interests or you are trying to influence large numbers of people (eg in a large change programme)	*Compliance/Commitment:* helps in breaking through a deadlock but runs risk of permanent polarization and future resistance from the losing or sidelined constituencies

Table 6.2 (contd)

6. *Rational argument:* presentation of the logic, cause-and-effect, expected outcomes. 'Let me explain the logic behind why we need to...'	In most circumstances, particularly stability and moderate change or where consensus is required, but not during crisis, threat of disaster and under conditions of 'learned helplessness'	*Commitment/Compliance:* important to get full consensus; requires a lot of communication; the logic of the argument needs to be underpinned by emotional engagement to produce more than short-term compliance
7. *Support:* praise, help, offers of assistance. 'You're doing a great job. If you need any help with...'	In circumstances of stability, moderate change, especially when building a new team	*Commitment:* creates a longer-term, sustained commitment that usually survives short- and medium-term difficulty and pressure
8. *Emotional engagement:* consultation, listening, exploring issues and needs, getting 'undiscussibles' out on the table. 'How do you feel about this? What are the issues getting in the way? How can we find a way through? What are your suggestions?'	Any time, except times of crisis	*Commitment:* builds trust between you and followers and is therefore crucial in broadening and sustaining your influence
9. *Catharsis:* creating space for emotional release – letting off steam, expressing frustrations, anger, fears and hopes. 'Be honest. Tell us how you feel. Get angry.'	During or after prolonged periods of organizational pressure, stress or lack of contact with leaders	*Commitment:* exposes resistance, releases energy and builds leader–follower trust. Best used via an objective third party
10. *Elevating ambition:* inspiring people to do more or better, to rise to a challenge or fulfil a destiny. 'We can change the industry! We can be the best.'	When transformation of your team/enterprise is required; during crisis; under threat of potential defeat or disaster	*Commitment:* requires you to have immense and obvious conviction to the cause and excellent oratory (oral and written); produces huge energy and action which need to be carefully directed

There are three guidelines for using influencing behaviours, discussed below.

1. Use the right influencing behaviours in the most appropriate circumstances

You need to take account of both potential short-term outcomes and longer-term implications. For example, constant over-reliance on pressure tactics may produce high performance and urgency today, tomorrow and next week, but will very likely be laying the foundations for an insidious culture of risk-aversion devoted to self-protection and inimical to team working and mutual support.

2. Don't over-rely on socially acceptable influencing behaviours

Some leaders make the mistake of relying on socially acceptable influencing behaviours such as support and rational argument because they don't want to upset people or so that they can avoid unpleasant decisions and confrontations. When such interventions fail, and then fail again, leaders are typically forced into follow-up interventions, each incrementally tougher and riskier than the last. Usually, the targets of the influencing attempt simply adjust to this incrementalism without changing their behaviour – a bit like the story of the frog that stubbornly gets boiled alive in a pot because the heat is turned up so gradually it doesn't notice. Worse still, such incrementalist approaches reflect badly on a leader. You look soft.

3. Decide whether you're aiming for commitment or compliance

Both are legitimate. But you should be pursuing them with different goals in mind.

Commitment engages the individual in *willingness to take responsibility and to add value*, for example, by innovating, going the extra mile for customers, making sacrifices for colleagues, the leader or the enterprise. Compliance secures the action intended by the leader but the result is that it *shifts the underlying responsibility straight back to the leader*. Your people will be thinking and feeling, 'I'm doing this because I have to, not because I want to.'

MODULE 6.3: TURN KNOWLEDGE INTO ACTION

One of the great enemies of successful enterprise is the inertia occasioned by habit, comfort and complacency. People become used to working in a settled way, doing the same things, often without question and without checking whether what they're doing is adding value to customers or to the enterprise. Their personal and corporate world seems secure and enjoyable. There is no compelling reason to really make things happen, to use information, to share knowledge, to change, or to make progress.

THE INERTIA TEST

Examine the everyday behaviour of your people in meetings – real-time, face-to-face, telephonic or virtual (intranet or internet based). Answer these questions:

- Do they know why they are meeting? What is their explicit purpose for the meeting?
- Do meetings generally run to time and reach a conclusion?
- Is there decision simplicity: in the form of yes or no or a choice between a, b, or c?
- Is there always someone designated to take a decision from the meeting?
- Are decisions designated a timescale, ie by when will this decision be made?
- Are individuals assigned responsibility for actions?
- Are actions to implement the decision designated a timescale (milestones and deadline)?

If you answer with hesitation or say 'No' to a number of these, then there is probably inertia in your enterprise, ie a failure to take action.

In the obverse, the Inertia Test is a set of guidelines for rapid decision-making and action.

Of course, decisions in meetings are just one dimension, but for human beings they play an enormously important role. Despite the meteoric rise of electronic media in facilitating decision-making, huge value is still placed on person-to-person 'meetings'. Indeed, as enterprise becomes more global, so organizations invest more in people travelling to meet one another as well as in the technological infrastructure to provide rapid communication and sharing of knowledge.

But, if knowledge (data, information and intelligence) is idle, then it becomes an opportunity cost to the enterprise. Around the world this is a multi-billion dollar cost. Ideas and information left sitting in the heads, the laptop files or desk drawers of thousands of people across an enterprise have the potential to transform ways of working, launch new products, offer added value to customers and save time – *but only if such ideas and information are turned into action*. More and more, this will be the challenge of leaders – to ensure that knowledge is shared and made to work.

Knowledge sharing can be facilitated by technology, but technology is often mistaken as *the* solution. Making heavy investments in technology results in an infrastructure that allows data and information to move; it does not guarantee that they *will* move; and it does not guarantee that they will be *used*. Thus, for senior executives it gives them a false cosy feeling of big bold action. It looks impressive, both inside and outside the organization. However, *information* is turned into *knowledge* by bringing disparate, often unconnected pieces of information together to create explicit options or alternatives. Evaluating these options and their implications provides the knowledge for taking decisions and then defining an agenda for action. Thus, knowledge is used and given value by taking *action*, as shown in Figure 6.1.

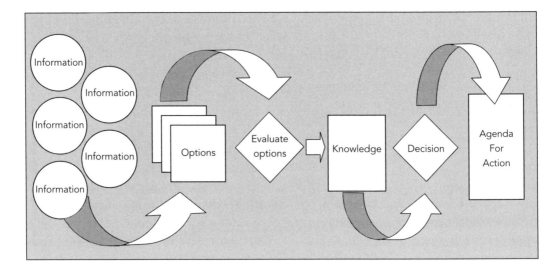

Figure 6.1   *Creating usefulness and value from information*

DIRECT LINE

In the British car insurance market in the late 1980s and 1990s, the entrepreneur Peter Wood created a new entrant, Direct Line. It carved out a 25 per cent share in less than a decade from start-up by combining pieces of information, built around a backbone of very simple technology – the telephone. The facts behind the success were:

- people tended to buy car insurance based on its cost (the cheapest price for the best cover);

- the dominant insurers, for historical reasons, had widespread insurance broking relationships, big branch networks and, as they discovered, concomitant high costs;

- an organization without the complex and costly infrastructure of branches and intermediary relationships with insurance brokers had, by comparison, very low overhead costs and could therefore pass big, attractive savings on to customers;

- people were comfortable making car insurance purchase decisions over a telephone and found it convenient.

Combined with smart mass marketing and rapid response, these different ideas actioned together captured large numbers of customers and, in a short time, transformed the nature of part of the insurance industry. However, the leadership lesson here, it is worth remembering, is that all the big insurers had the same information. It took an outsider to the industry to put the pieces together.

Turning knowledge into action (or turning what you know into what you do) requires five main actions, discussed below.

1. Make explicit who takes the decisions

The density of corporate fog constantly amazes me: who really has the responsibility to take decisions? Sometimes the organizational design is wrong and too many people have decision-making responsibility; some of the worst instances are where a committee or other body is charged with decision-making and no one individual makes the call. Sometimes the culture makes decision-making processes slippery and it's hard to know who gives the final yes or no. Whatever the case, this represents a failure of leadership.

Make it your priority to clear the lines of decision-making. Always identify single-point accountability, especially within committees, in project teams or task forces that span departments and functions. If this means changing organizational structures, do it. If you don't have the authority, assert your leadership or use your influence to do it.

2. Push decision-making as far down the hierarchy as possible

As a leader you will never have enough access to information to pull even a fraction of the critical decisions up to you and keep the enterprise running. Where organizational hierarchies suck authority and decisions up to the highest levels, it typically follows that the organization is sluggish, lumbering and under-performing. The best leaders do the opposite. Give your people the space, opportunity and support to take their own decisions. Don't just throw responsibility and autonomy away, but devolve it systematically as a matter of practice. People will then come to expect it. Judge people on the basis of their willingness and success in decision-making.

Remember also that people's decision-making is only as good as the information they have and the options or alternatives they identify. Defining explicit alternatives forces managers to make more coherent decisions by understanding the implications or consequences of each.

3. Place value on 'can do' action over planning, analysing, meeting, thinking

Most enterprises tend to slow action down. Often organizational consequences punish action while ignoring or even, bizarrely, rewarding inaction. This is the 'keep your head down and your nose clean' syndrome. Moreover, organizational rules and administrative systems can become corporate treacle that retard action or that get used as excuses for tardiness or inaction. But leaders need to get things done, to make things happen – and they get things done and make things happen through other people taking action. Make it clear that you value action over and above everything else. Likewise, make it clear that you do not value 'busyness' for its own sake – busyness such as lots of meetings, endless planning, discussions, analysis and so on. Certainly these things are important but action in pursuit of a defined purpose – ie the context you impose – is what leaders require.

One of the best ways to make this real is to expect your people to develop an agenda for action – clearly articulated – that specifies what must be done, by whom and when. This agenda specifies the priorities for where you commit time, resource, investment and effort. By implication therefore the agenda should force your people away from committing time, resources, investment and effort into other things. In other words, the agenda channels energy towards your context or purpose.

4. Clear obstacles and barriers out of the way

Anything that slows people down or gets in the way of their making progress on what needs to be done is incredibly frustrating and stifles motivation. You know what gets in the way and, if you don't, find out. Get your people to tell you: engage with them about the barriers and obstacles that affect their work. Look especially for common themes where you can leverage your effort for maximum impact – eg processes with bottle-necks that restrict the efforts of key people or teams; administrative bureaucracy that could be adjusted or swept away; ridiculous rules that still exist for historical reasons.

Don't try to understand and develop solutions to the barriers yourself: you will drown in the swamp. Get the people who have to live with the barriers and obstacles to define the changes and, wherever possible, make the changes themselves. They generally know best, even though they may need your leadership sanction to make changes. Followers tend to be impressed by leaders who make the time and invest the effort to help their people: this builds trust.

5. Create urgency

The notion of e-speed has become popular recently, but leaders have been emphasizing urgency for considerably longer than that – at least since the dawn of civilization. A palpable sense of urgency itself creates action and gets people to start to draw on information in order to make decisions which themselves galvanize people to further action. The way to generate this sense of urgency is to:

- set stretching goals and deadlines;

- make clear who is accountable and make sure it is single-point accountability, ie a named individual, not a group or committee;

- be clear that a deadline is a deadline and should not be missed, ie set unequivocal expectations;

- put in place intermediate milestones *en route* to the main deadline in order to concentrate attention on progressive goals and thereby set the pace early and sustain it. If you don't you'll get the *late bulge effect* – the need for a rush of activity and effort in the last stage before the deadline, but insufficient and too late to achieve your goal;

- get regular progress updates.

MODULE 6.4: STAY THE COURSE

As they become more complex – through size, scale, speed, alliances, mergers and globalization – so most enterprises face the problem of starting initiatives and not finishing them. People lose interest or hit difficult obstacles. Sometimes, business-as-usual takes precedence. Or managers identify projects and initiatives that must be launched to get the original initiatives back on track. Or the environment changes in some way – new people, a new competitor, poor results, extra work-load – and a different spin is put on the shape or direction of key initiatives. Typically, project proliferation and general busyness come to substitute for purpose and real progress. As a leader, your original goal is being eroded by a false sense of action. Your own role (as set out in Module 3.4) should be concerned with getting your people to ask questions about:

- why an initiative should go ahead or continue (even if it's been running for months or years);
- what its importance is against other initiatives;
- how it fits with finances, not only this year but also one and two years from now;
- how (and this is the clincher) it contributes to overall direction or purpose.

If you suspect that there is too much action without much progress in your team, you probably have to pull the plug on some initiatives (see Module 3.4). You certainly have to get better at follow-through, with sufficient determination and courage to stick to a specific effort long enough so that it works and pays off. Quite often this will be in the face of frustration, boredom, anxiety or even resistance by your people.

However, staying the course achieves two things. First, it ensures that real progress is made on a few key initiatives or against a number of goals critical to your overall purpose, instead of dissipating effort across too many fronts and therefore always being late or underperforming. Second, it builds commitment from your people in the longer term: they will see that half-measures, distractions and giving up on difficult or unfinished business are not tolerated. Waverers are more likely to stiffen their resolve and resistors to acknowledge that the way things are moving might make them isolated or leave them behind.

One neat leadership technique for driving results in the short term on key priorities is the *4 by 4 by 4* tool:

- *Set a 4-month timeline.* The anticipated work must have a goal of being completed within four months and must deliver. Subsequent work can be scheduled, but it too should be on another four-month timeline. This concentrates attention and makes the time horizon close enough to drive urgency and results.

- *Task 4 people to tackle the work.* They should work as a team and can use additional resources, but those four remain the core, responsible team with one of them taking single-point accountability. Limiting the team to four makes communication, goal understanding and teamwork considerably easier but allows a sufficient number to be able to work together to make progress.

- *Demand results/payback within 4 months.* Make it clear that you expect an agreed set of specified benefits, results or payback to accrue within four months of the end of the work. This concentrates effort, not on activities (ie busyness), but on behaviour that produces tangible results.

This sort of approach works extremely well where a leader faces multiple demands and high expectations that progress will be made. Think of the demands as bundles or chunks rather than one great, complex lump. Slice the lump up into smaller bundles and apply the 4 by 4 by 4 tool. Sceptical managers object that using four people is hopelessly inadequate for some of the mega-projects or issues facing them in their organizations. Correct. But this is not a prescription for just four people to tackle a billion-dollar infrastructure implementation. The tool allows the four-person team to draw on resources but it limits the core, responsible team to a performance-optimizing number who can solve problems, communicate and make decisions fast. Most important, the tool focuses attention and effort on a manageable chunk of work, thereby multiplying the probability of success.

UNCOMFORTABLE LEADERSHIP LESSON NO. 7.
DEVELOP YOUR PEOPLE AS YOU DEVELOP YOURSELF

Jennifer is a highly successful entrepreneur running an internet business that she built from scratch, almost bankrupting herself twice in the process. When she started out she had only six or seven people working for her and things were tough. But her perseverance held out and, as her employees would say, 'She believed in something that we could all believe in.' In that respect she was inspirational. Her team were able to stick with her during the hard months and they all forged a strong bond of loyalty and support, learning new skills rapidly as the enterprise required them. Because the business was still young, everyone pitched in to help on just about anything. Of course, after 18 months, with rapid growth and dozens of new recruits, it was obvious they needed to create specialist roles, particularly in finance and marketing, if the business was to continue to thrive.

Jennifer handled most of the finance with support from one of her original employees, but she felt out of her depth on the marketing front. She gathered four of her people together regularly to tackle the issue between them, but it was frustrating: the effort was out of proportion to the results; they weren't winning the business Jennifer wanted to win; she felt they were sliding backwards. She began to feel that each of the members of the close-knit original team was limited and would not be able to give her the bedrock of support she really needed for going forward. Her frustration was obvious to her team. One of them, Andy, offered to take on the marketing role, saying that he would learn as he went along. Jennifer decided against it. She felt she had waited too long already. Impatient to get on, she was now convinced that they needed a hotshot marketing professional in post – fast. Andy, of course, was hugely disappointed but Jennifer was determined.

After three months of advertising, job interviews and worry, Jennifer appointed the person she thought was exactly right for their needs. His CV was impressive, he interviewed well and she believed he would get on well with her team, even though he was obviously better qualified and would, in her view, soon outstrip them, probably becoming one of the core team who would help her run the business in the future. She was pleased and excited.

Unfortunately, matters didn't work out quite as she had anticipated. The new man had ideas, but they were unworkable in Jennifer's business because he didn't really understand the market. Within six months they had made no significant progress – nine months after deciding to get someone into the role. The situation was intolerable. She was impatient, angry, hesitant to make a decision and losing sleep. Moreover, though at first she would not admit it to herself, it soon dawned on her that she had alienated her original, loyal team, as well as many of her other people. There was nothing overt, but the powerful motivation and commitment she unthinkingly relied on had eroded somewhat. Initially, she got angry. Who did they think they were? She had given them their chance. What did they expect from her? She had to grow this business or it would die. None the less, the situation remained. She had to make a decision. For the first time ever, she felt that she might actually have screwed up so badly as to damage the business.

Then, during a conversation over lunch, a friend commented, 'Perhaps Andy and the others feel you could have given one of them the same opportunity you gave this new marketing guy – you know, to prove themselves, even if they couldn't handle it in the end.' A light went on in Jennifer's head. Things fell into place. She had turned down Andy's offer to take on the marketing role and therefore to develop his skills and contribute to the further growth of the business. In effect she had sent a signal to Andy, her core team and the rest of the firm that they would not be able to develop with the business, even if they had the ambition and courage to take on difficult challenges. Furthermore, she had lost a precious nine months during which time Andy might have made huge strides in getting to grips with the marketing.

The decision to let the marketing guy go was a no-brainer. Far more uncomfortable – and profound, as she came to realize – was the lesson that while she had to hire new people to grow the business, she likewise had an unquestionable duty to develop her team and everyone else in the business. The enterprise itself could not develop without the ongoing development of its human assets. The alternative was a constant and expensive battle to find new talent and implement complex devices to sustain motivation and morale.

Two years later, Jennifer's business had grown 20-fold, Andy was Head of Marketing and most of her original team held key executive positions. The leadership lesson of developing people around her is still the most important lesson of her career.

MODULE 6.5: CREATE AND SUSTAIN AN ETHOS OF HUMAN DEVELOPMENT

Microsoft is credited with making every effort to hire the best people, develop them and retain them. General Electric has a reputation for nurturing people over time, through top-notch training and experiential development, so that the company has a huge pool of talent available. In both cases, the value created by the enterprise is directly driven by the value of the people.

This was not always the case. For most of the 20th century, value was driven by capital and machines. Indeed, machines were invented, developed and plugged in with the explicit aim of doing the work of people faster, better and cheaper. Luddite reactions to machines and new technology – from the Industrial Revolution in England in the 18th century until the 21st century – have always been short-lived. Though the replacement of people by machines has been painful for those most directly affected, inevitably the use of machines in myriad industries has created the conditions for people to do other kinds of work. In recent times, it has meant they can engage in huge new industries devoted to the creation of new technologies such as computer hardware, software, telecommunications and e-business.

At the beginning of the 21st century, though there is still poverty, war and the grind of exploitative and poorly paid work for many, there is also an unprecedented kaleidoscope of work options open to billions of people all over the world. Our era and our social existence demand products, service and ideas of a sophistication and at a scale unparalleled in history. And it is people once again, not machines, that are at the heart of creating, fashioning and delivering these things.

In parallel with this trend, as the globalizing marketplace has grown rapidly, so the demand for talented people has accelerated. Skills are in short supply and the best companies snap them up. In this milieu it is easy for highly skilled people to become *talent nomads*, skipping from job to job or becoming *contingent workers* who charge themselves out as free agents, thus maximizing their pay, their job satisfaction and the enjoyment of their home life. Moreover, recruiting talented people from a shrinking global talent pool is time-consuming, expensive and has a low probability of success.

These factors have created interesting and complex challenges for leaders. In one very important way, leaders no longer have control over their people like their predecessors might have had. Workers can more easily leave, especially the most talented or those with specialist skills, or they are already working on a contingent basis and therefore your relationship with them will be short-lived and arm's-length. In addition, it is hardly an option, in the shrinking talent pool described above, to simply buy in skills as required. Needless to say, the leadership of people under these conditions is different.

One of the central thrusts of leadership has always been the development of people, for two reasons. First, there is a need to build a depth of skills behind leaders to strengthen the enterprise and lead others in turn. Second, a pool of potential leaders to take on the succession at an appropriate time is required.

This thrust has an added impetus nowadays: given the economic and social backdrop painted above, leaders must devote a high proportion of their time and effort to building the ethos for skills development within their enterprise, and specifically for all the following reasons:

- With a shortage of talent in the market, you cannot rely on recruitment to help feed an expanding enterprise; you must grow the skills of your existing work-force.

- Talented people are more likely to be retained by the enterprise if they have the opportunities to learn and develop and are given the time to do so.

- Skill development sustained over time encourages workforce loyalty and commitment to the enterprise.

- Innovation is becoming more and more important in the organizational and business world – for survival, success and future growth – and innovation is fired by the interaction of skilled people.

- You have to develop as broad and deep a base of high-level human perfor-mance as possible if you are to generate real critical mass, ie get as many people as possible doing the right things fast and effectively.

Self-evidently there are numerous activities that are important in developing the human performance asset base of your enterprise – competency identification, training, management development, performance management and so on. But these are management actions. While leaders must be sure that the appropriate infrastructure is in place to develop people, their most important role is to *create and sustain the ethos or climate for human development* so that people:

- are motivated to develop their knowledge and skills;
- continue to develop their skills rather than being satisfied with how far they've developed or how much they've learnt;
- want to contribute their knowledge and skills to the enterprise.

Building the ethos for human development means that you need to be active in the following ways:

1. Make people feel valued.
2. Expose people to developmental experiences.
3. Give people space to succeed and grow.
4. Develop a number of potential successors.

1. Make people feel valued

Take the time and invest the effort in giving people recognition for their work and achievements. This requires you to be close enough to their work to understand and know what they're doing and what they've achieved. By contrast, blanket stock phrases such as, 'Thank you for all your efforts this year' have little impact; they are polite but nothing more. Recognition works when it is personal, ie directed at specific individuals or teams for specific achievements. Any reward, recognition included, works best when it is specific. If you find it uncomfortable or embarrassing to thank people directly or tell them they've done a good job, then write a note, send an e-mail or arrange to send a gift such as champagne or flowers. Alternatively, give people some time off that is in addition to their normal leave allowance.

Furthermore, the simple action of spending time *listening* to your people (and *showing* you are listening) can, both in the short term and over time, be immensely powerful in motivating individuals. In the short term it enables people to get out their frustrations and deal with underlying problems; in the longer term it builds trust and commitment. So, go out and talk to your people. Leaders use methods such as:

- scheduled but informal lunches to discuss work issues;

- workshops, run by an objective facilitator, to get directly at concerns or barriers, which are reported back to the leader;

- walking the office or getting out to people's locations to listen and learn about the circumstances in which they operate;

- regular roadshows to communicate information and to take questions.

Also, make sure you tell your people, from time to time, how they individually fit into the context and purpose you have set and how they can contribute. This makes real the connection between the effort and actions of many individuals and the direction or goals that bind them together to make things happen.

Finally, let your people take the glory for their achievements – *never* steal their glory. Too many leaders develop this fatal flaw and, ultimately, are tripped up by it. They begin to imagine that it is only owing to their own brilliance that they are successful. They forget that leaders are both masters and servants: they say how things should be, but serve their people in helping to fulfil their goal.

2. Expose people to developmental experiences

Go out of your way to give people opportunities to try out their skills. This is not a task to be delegated to some internal department or to other individuals, although clearly that is helpful. Leaders should take the lead in helping others to build their skills. It is in this way that leaders safeguard the future of the enterprise and enhance its current capacity to thrive. Take risks with people, too. Human development is not, in fact, a gently rising learning curve of gradually increasing knowledge and skill – it is a series of uneven steps, triggered by environmental challenges in which people learn new skills. Some options are:

- Give someone additional responsibility in a current role.

- Promote someone earlier than they expect.
- Ask individuals or teams to set their own goals, with the proviso that they stretch those goals so that they learn new knowledge or skills.
- Set short-term projects in new areas of expertise for specific individuals.
- Get young managers or executives to take on external or non-executive board appointments in smaller firms or subsidiaries to learn board-level skills early in their career.
- Offer regular advice or coaching as people tackle new areas or levels of responsibility.
- Allow mistakes or failure, but spend time, in a truly open and trusting manner, helping people learn from failure.

3. Give people space to succeed and grow

It has been said that the best leaders select a talented bunch of people, set the goal and broad parameters and then get out of the way. There is much truth in this. If you micromanage you will get short-term results for the loss of longer-term motivation, sense of responsibility and the commitment to innovate and learn. Tight micromanagement is sensible in times of crisis or corporate turnaround (see Module 6.2) to pressure people into immediate compliance with a defined array of necessary actions. However, the complexity of modern, networked enterprises and the pressure for e-speed preclude a static workforce: if your people are not learning new skills and knowledge, then your enterprise as a whole will rapidly fall behind. People on the ground, at the customer interface, usually know what skills they need, though they may not know how to structure the resource to acquire such skills. Listen to them, therefore, and ensure that the infrastructure exists to support their learning.

4. Develop a number of potential successors

It is a sad flaw of many leaders that they fail to really develop successors. This ultimately leaves them with a problem and the longer it is left, the more serious the problem. Too often, leaders end up faced with serious external difficulties and an absence of effective or credible leadership successors when they should already have passed on the mantle to up-and-coming leaders. On such occasions, nine times out of ten, leaders plunge to a disastrous end. Being aware of the problem, many certainly struggle with it, but few get it right. There are a number of factors that conspire against leaders, not least:

- their own self-belief (ie arrogance) that no one else can take their place;

- the tendency to cast a long shadow – to be so prominent and powerful that they do not allow potential successors to develop;

- the fear of being deposed by a younger, better, more charismatic leader;

- a heartfelt desire to keep going because they are still successful, thereby getting in the way of successors when the time is right for a change in leadership;

- the mistake of identifying a single 'crown prince' successor whose disappointed colleagues then conspire to make sure he or she fails, trips up or is isolated.

In developing appropriate succession, you need to be active in testing and developing potential leaders against the toughest challenges. So, on the one hand, you must be identifying the best possible successors and, on the other, testing them for stepping into the senior leadership role. Here are some ways of doing this:

- Be clear on the criteria for leadership and start to identify those potential successors who show leadership.

- Task the small group of people you have identified with handling the most demanding customer segments.

- Ask them to take on roles or projects in the most difficult teams, departments or business units.

- Give them the toughest assignments, especially those that involve leading change or that demand new thinking and approaches.

- Load up their leadership responsibility, for example additional project roles or larger teams.

- Decide on the right time to pass over the leadership succession and stick to it.

Course summary

Generating critical mass is concerned with influencing people and turning knowledge into action in order to channel your people's energy into the appropriate activities, mobilize all your people to work together in a coordinated way (rather than in an individualistic, haphazard manner) and make things happen:

1. Use influencing tactics to get commitment or compliance.

2. Turn knowledge into action by pushing decision-making down the hierarchy, placing value on action and urgency and clearing barriers out of your people's way.

3. Stay the course, persevere and finish what you start.

4. Build an ethos of human development so that people are motivated to improve their knowledge and skills and want to contribute these to the growth of the enterprise.

7 The dominant leadership sub-domains

Key action list and course objectives

- To understand how underlying personality, psychological preferences, knowledge and skills, and the environment interact to drive particular patterns of leadership behaviour.

- To identify the main sub-domains of leadership behaviour.

- To pinpoint your own dominant leadership pattern.

- To challenge yourself to deal with blind spots and weaknesses.

MODULE 7.1: DOMINANT LEADERSHIP PATTERNS

As you have worked your way through each of the preceding courses, you will have built up a profile of yourself as a leader. The progress checklists will have given you a measure of whether each of the five areas is a strength or not. For example, you may find that you have deep conviction, are able to impose context and generate critical mass. On the other hand, you may feel uncomfortable about making and taking risks and shy away from challenging and changing things. This is a fairly typical pattern and is described further in this course, together with six other patterns or sub-domains of leadership.

These patterns arise from the interaction of several things. First, as you develop from childhood to adult life, your personality becomes more or less fixed. Psychologists have identified what have come to be called the 'Big Five' personality traits. So you may tend to be extrovert (outward-looking, getting your energy from the world around you and the people in it) or introvert (more inwardly focused, preferring time to yourself and taking your energy from the inner world of thoughts and ideas). Moreover, you may be good-natured, eager to cooperate and avoid conflict or, on the other hand, hard-headed, sceptical and competitive. The other three remaining personality traits fix people in a range from being sensitive and emotional to secure and relaxed, open and imaginative to practical and set in your ways, and lastly conscientious and well organized to easygoing and preferring not to make plans.

Second, the experiences you have, particularly in the early formative years of your life, afford you opportunities, some welcome, some unpalatable, that forge a preference to behave in certain ways in specific types of situation – like your willingness to experiment or take risks. Typically, if the consequences of taking risks at school and in your early years were positive and paid off, you will be more likely to experiment and take risks in other endeavours later in life, such as taking on opportunities for promotion, overseas assignments or starting a business. By contrast, experiences with emotionally negative consequences or a series of setbacks can create risk-aversion or a tendency towards extreme caution.

Third, the knowledge and skills you acquire from school, training, college, university and so on will equip you with extra 'tools' to be effective in the world, with the added benefit that your confidence is boosted. This is particularly true in any competitive arena, like business, where the latest knowledge and skills can have an advantage both for the individual (in making them better at their job) and for the organization (in delivering increased value to customers and shareholders).

All of these factors interact together to make people who they are. To take this a step further, it is therefore self-evident that to become highly effective as a leader, individuals must understand where they are strong, where they are weak, what their preferences are and what they seek to avoid, where they feel confident and where exposed, and which situations suit them best or least. The seven leadership sub-domains set out in this course are a way for you to understand what your dominant pattern of leadership is – in other words, where you will have greatest impact and add greatest leadership value.

MODULE 7.2: THE LEADERSHIP SUB-DOMAINS

The Transformational Leader

Leaders who show strength in all the components of the leadership domain are those who are able to transform the commitment levels of those around them, to get their unit or their organization to create breakpoint advantages, open up new opportunities and even reinvent whole markets. Figure 7.1 displays this: if you

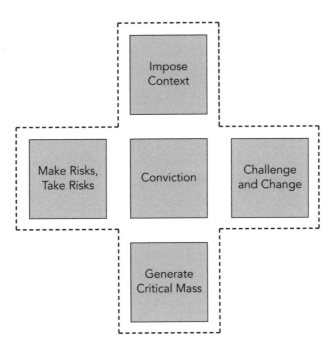

Figure 7.1   *The Transformational Leader*

have genuine strengths in all the five components, you are a rare breed, you have unique leadership advantages and you create unique value around you.

THE TRANSFORMATIONAL LEADER: CHARACTERISTICS

- deep conviction about what they want to achieve;

- preparedness to go against conventional wisdom;

- surround themselves with followers who demonstrate a range of outlooks – commitment to execution and delivery, unorthodox thinking and creativity, willingness to challenge;

- restless energy to push others to get things right, to aspire to more;

- determination to make things happen, to execute on plans;

- clear about the agenda for decisions and action;

- able to unite multiple constituencies around inspirational goals;

- seek out opportunities to make convictions and aspirations real;

- unlikely to be put off by short-term or even persistent setbacks;

- inspire through logic and appeals to shared ambition: 'We can achieve our aspirations if, collectively, we stick to our ambition and deliver more than we have before!';

- rarely prevaricate, ruthless follow-through;

- encourage autonomy in others to seek opportunities, take risks and execute plans.

The Enforcer

These are leaders who act in ways characterized by cautious optimism and a drive to make sure that specific objectives are achieved, for example that the strategic goals of the enterprise or business unit are enforced. Figure 7.2 shows that they are strong down the vertical axis of the domain but weak in making and taking risks and in challenge and change. If this is your profile, you will display strong belief in what you are doing and commitment to stay the course. You will have a preference for the steady state, be excellent at setting clear direction and making it all happen in an organized way. However, you will tend to limit options (even if these create attractive opportunities) in order to maintain your control over the primary goal. You will also avoid committing to action on anything with even limited risk attached, preferring to surround yourself with committed, disciplined followers who demonstrate their ability to deliver the agreed plan. Generally you will be unconvinced that change to your unit or the organization at large is desirable, but when you are convinced and you feel you have control, you will pursue the new direction or goal with the same optimistic dedication.

Figure 7.2   *The Enforcer*

THE ENFORCER: CHARACTERISTICS

- clear on direction, context and the agenda for action;
- strong belief in what they want to achieve and commitment to make it happen;
- dedicated to successful achievement and unity around the objective: 'This is our goal; let's achieve it together.';
- prefer direct control over the plan and its execution;
- dislike being challenged;
- focus on detail and analysis;
- wary of risk and risk-takers;
- perturbed by change and will generally avoid it or try to control it;
- tend to prefer centralized structures and to keep team and followers on a tight rein;
- uncomfortable with multiple options; prefer limited parameters where the goal is clear;
- danger of underachieving through restriction of possibilities and ambition;
- will do well in stable situations, with limited competitive threat.

The Deal Maker

Deal Makers are leaders who attract followers largely because of their energy and obsession with the excitement of anything new. They thrive on change and bring this to life by seeking out or creating opportunities. In the business world, they often rise to prominence on the back of their reputation for the deals they pull off. Because they are adept at challenging norms and accepted wisdom, they frequently break the mould and are innovative and exciting leaders. Moreover, risk-taking is their lifeblood and this attracts others with similar outlook, triggering a culture around the leader which has few mechanisms of control and cool analysis with which to counterbalance the forces of risk and adventure.

Bored easily, they want to move on, with little regard for the legacy they might leave, the nature of the enterprise they might create or the damage they might do by not following through to sustain success in the very thing they have created. As shown in Figure 7.3, their lack of conviction, except where it concerns the pursuit of the new and exciting, usually gets them into difficulties – they may have no moral compass to guide their decisions and actions.

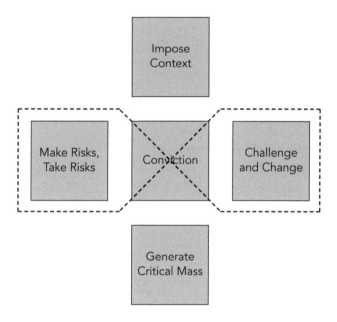

Figure 7.3   *The Deal Maker*

THE DEAL MAKER: CHARACTERISTICS

- excellent at breaking the mould and trying new things;
- narrow motivational focus on the excitement of the new or different;

- obsessed with goals that, below a veneer of conviction, are chiefly self-serving;

- are not above shading the truth and distorting the facts to suit their own ends or win the argument;

- get bored easily;

- often talented at building businesses from small beginnings through multiple acquisitions;

- attract followers who gain from access to new challenges and opportunities;

- inspire loyalty and hard work because of their sense of adventure and willingness to experiment;

- tend to ignore or reject those who counsel caution or delay;

- have little interest in building, only in securing short-term 'wins' or 'deals';

- avoid detail and analysis and usually casually delegate these;

- can be a disruptive influence in stable enterprises that need to focus on delivery.

The Administrator

These leaders are similar to the Enforcer, but lack deep conviction (see Figure 7.4). This means that they can be excellent 'doers' or 'strategic executors' who are crystal clear about what needs to be achieved and then ruthlessly follow through. They are autocratic in approach, letting nothing stand in the way of the overall objective, and are likely to prefer detailed and rigorous project plans, constant monitoring and updating and tight control over resources and people. They get things done but only through generating compliance. Followers never put in more effort than is required and will not sacrifice self-interest for the good of this leader. The Administrator is therefore a transactional leader – rewarding followers for success in completing stated objectives. This is fine until the onset of difficult times or setbacks. In these circumstances the Administrator is likely to face scepticism, uncooperative passivity or even outright resistance. These leaders have little tolerance for risk-takers, innovators or those with new or different approaches to offer, chiefly because these types of people tend to disrupt short-term execution of the 'plan', even if long-term advantages may accrue from using and building on new ideas. As a result, the scope of their leadership is limited and primarily effective in narrowly defined parameters. They are thus likely to under-perform in senior executive roles.

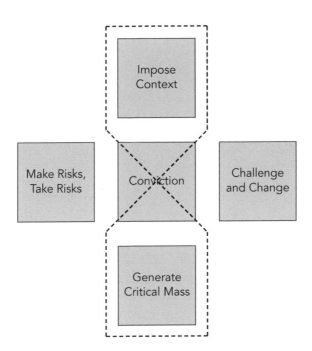

Figure 7.4   *The Administrator*

THE ADMINISTRATOR: CHARACTERISTICS

- excellent in delivery roles (they make things happen, on time and at all costs);

- autocratic, unyielding, committed to seeing things through;
- the 'plan' for execution is more important than anything else;
- narrow focus on execution and delivery makes them blind to options and possibilities;
- prefer strong direct control over resources and people; dislike decentralized organizational structures;
- handle change by forcing the 'plan' through the change, even at high personal and resource cost;
- viewed by others as impersonal and uninspiring because they have or display little conviction;
- operate in a transactional way: 'If you do what the plan requires, you will be rewarded.'

The Visionary

These leaders can be both immensely exciting and desperately frustrating. They have all of the qualities of transformational leaders, including their ability to elevate ambition, but are weak in generating critical mass (Figure 7.5). They inspire people to dream of greatness but frequently seem hesitant or uninterested in follow-through. They paint extraordinary visions of future ambition, uniting followers in the collective pursuit of high ideals, yet fail to channel energy into the actions that matter. Where they are most successful is where they recognize their own shortcomings and either appoint a loyal deputy, superb at marshalling people and resources to the right ends, or build around them a strong team capable of executing their vision. By contrast, at their worst, their inspirational leadership draws in the enterprise to commit to lofty goals in a fanfare of idealistic public excitement, only to fall tragically short.

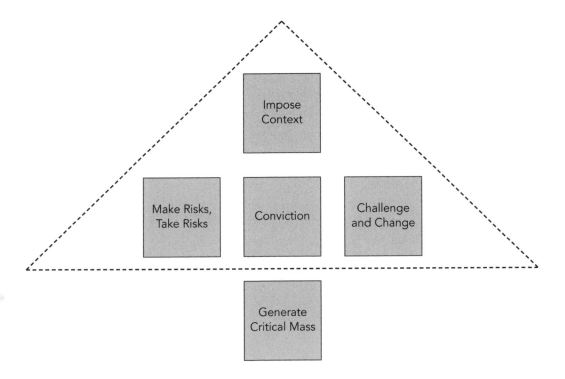

Figure 7.5   *The Visionary*

THE VISIONARY: CHARACTERISTICS

- deep interest in future possibilities and multiple options;

- tend to be conceptual, focus on big ideas;

- love and become absorbed in the detail and complexity of concepts and ideas;

- grab people's attention because of their evident excitement and passion for an idea or aspiration;

- tend to see and present difficulties as opportunities – unquenchably optimistic;

- in times of crisis or setbacks, offer bold new ideas and alternatives as solutions and may therefore be seen as brilliant strategists;

- need a loyal, robust and understanding deputy who can translate concepts and ambitions rapidly into implementable action;

- find it hard to concentrate on the practicalities of, and obstacles to, executing plans;

- can neglect short-term exigencies while their gaze is on the long-term and bigger picture;

- often prefer entrepreneurial roles, where there is the excitement of building a business or something new.

The Serial Entrepreneur

These are the leaders who are very strong across the horizontal axis of the domain (Figure 7.6). They are imaginative, but calculating, gamblers. They want to create opportunities that they believe in and see them come to fruition. In pursuing these opportunities they display huge energy and commitment, sweeping people along with them because they make seemingly impossible challenges achievable. Their interest is not in steady state or stable enterprises: they thrive on change and creating change. Once they have created the institution or the business that they aimed for, at that point they will often hand the reins to a trusted deputy. Trust figures highly for them: because they commit so much of themselves to the goals they pursue, they want others to do the same. They care deeply about their legacy. They are therefore very different to the Deal Maker leaders, whose interest in the thing they create goes no further than the adventure of making it happen.

However, it is sometimes hard for followers to see where this leader is going. The only guide is usually the leader's convictions. Where they are successful it is where deputies or a team are able to tie their leader's convictions and interests

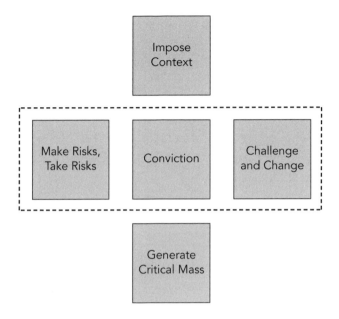

Figure 7.6 *The Serial Entrepreneur*

together and articulate the wider context in a meaningful way. Moreover, whilst leaders who are Serial Entrepreneurs are fun to be around, their dislike of routine and of the detail of implementation means they get bored quickly. They would identify strongly with George Bernard Shaw's remark: 'Consistency is the first refuge of the unimaginative.'

THE SERIAL ENTREPRENEUR: CHARACTERISTICS

- generate excitement for the things they care about;
- thrive on change and making change happen;
- imaginative, often innovators in one or a number of fields;

- unite people in aspirational goals because of the force of their convictions;

- rely on trusting others to help them achieve their goals and leave a legacy;

- attract followers who gain from access to new challenges and opportunities;

- dislike routine and detail of implementation;

- ignore those who counsel caution or delay unless the issue or action they are contemplating conflicts with their own convictions;

- 'It can't be done,' drives them to say, 'I must do it.'

The Spin Doctor

These are the leaders who seem to be everything a leader should be, but whose behaviour often seems inconsistent, self-serving or even at times downright corrupt. As shown in Figure 7.7, such leaders have underdeveloped conviction. They do everything else with aplomb. They can motivate large numbers of people through their apparent espousal of direction and aspirational goals. They are bold in creating opportunities and decisive in action. They are prepared to challenge conventional wisdom and accepted notions and push for real change. They organize superbly and channel effort to make things happen. But... people are always slightly uncomfortable with these leaders. They sense the absence of a moral centre. What at first seems an undoubted commitment of the leader to a core of things that matter, later seems to be swept aside or is seen to have been sham. It is not that the leader seems to lack any less self-belief, but rather that he or she can so swiftly move from one conviction to another, even if the shift is one of extremes. What distinguishes these leaders most, however, is their ability to convincingly argue the case, any case, and justify the change to followers. If they do not move on first, such leaders are brought to account or pushed out of office when followers at last become convinced that at the heart of these individuals is overwhelming self-interest – leadership for them is important only in how it ultimately serves their own personal needs and ambitions.

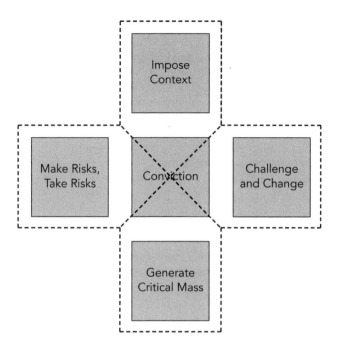

Figure 7.7   *The Spin Doctor*

This sub-domain of leadership is particularly dangerous when such individuals are at the top of enterprises. This happens when the CEOs of large businesses use their authority, power and organizational resources to pursue actions which actually serve their own personal agenda rather than that of the institution – for example, chasing down high-profile acquisitions or driving through mega-mergers in order to make their mark or secure their place in corporate history.

THE SPIN DOCTOR: CHARACTERISTICS

- capable leaders in the short-term;

- self-interest at the heart of their leadership behaviour;
- make decisions inconsistently: on the basis of rational, economic or business logic but often overlaid with a keen eye for how it will bolster their own position, status, wealth or advancement;
- confident and self-assured;
- attract followers through their self-assurance and charm, but typically fall out with many of them in time;
- usually articulate, convincing and capable influencers;
- are not above shading the truth and distorting the facts to suit their own ends or win the argument;
- tend to move on before their self-interest brings them to account;

Index

NB: page numbers in *italic* indicate figures or tables